Praise for *Connected by Design*

"R/GA has remained ahead of its competition by reinventing itself, and R/GA's newest transformation is designed to help brands achieve functional integration. *Connected by Design* outlines how brands like Nike, Google, Amazon, Apple, and McCormick have grown with functional integration and why you'll want to consider it for your brand."

— **Rick Boyko**, former director, Virginia Commonwealth University Brandcenter; former chief creative officer, Ogilvy North America

"If you have ever wondered about the secret to the enormous success of companies such as Apple, Google, Nike, and Amazon, *Connected by Design* is for you. This engaging and readable book explains the functional integration business model of these companies. It's a must-read for understanding how to survive and grow in the dynamic and complex age of networks and ecosystems."

— **Jerry Wind**, The Lauder Professor, The Wharton School

"Brands that aren't rethinking how to connect their products, services, and communications are leaving brand equity on the table. Functional integration is a great playbook for creating and capturing brand value in the digital age."

— **John Gerzema**, chairman and CEO, BAV Consulting, and author, *The Athena Doctrine*

"*Connected by Design* represents the business course you never took but should have taken, and the design class you never had but now wish you did. It prepares your mind and way of thinking for this high-speed world, where more and more value is delivered in the form of digital experiences. Barry Wacksman and Chris Stutzman take you deep into leading companies and share their guiding principles."

— **Keith Yamashita**, chairman, SY/Partners and SY/Products

Connected
by Design

w

Connected by Design

7 Principles of Business Transformation
Through Functional Integration

Barry Wacksman and Chris Stutzman

JB JOSSEY-BASS™

A Wiley Brand

Published by Jossey-Bass
A Wiley Brand
One Montgomery Street, Suite 1200, San Francisco, CA 94104-4594—www.josseybass.com

Limit of Liability/Disclaimer of Warranty: While the publisher and author have used their best efforts in preparing this book, they make no representations or warranties with respect to the accuracy or completeness of the contents of this book and specifically disclaim any implied warranties of merchantability or fitness for a particular purpose. No warranty may be created or extended by sales representatives or written sales materials. The advice and strategies contained herein may not be suitable for your situation. You should consult with a professional where appropriate. Neither the publisher nor author shall be liable for any loss of profit or any other commercial damages, including but not limited to special, incidental, consequential, or other damages. Readers should be aware that Internet Web sites offered as citations and/or sources for further information may have changed or disappeared between the time this was written and when it is read.

Jossey-Bass books and products are available through most bookstores. To contact Jossey-Bass directly call our Customer Care Department within the U.S. at 800-956-7739, outside the U.S. at 317-572-3986, or fax 317-572-4002.

Wiley publishes in a variety of print and electronic formats and by print-on-demand. Some material included with standard print versions of this book may not be included in e-books or in print-on-demand. If this book refers to media such as a CD or DVD that is not included in the version you purchased, you may download this material at **http://booksupport.wiley.com**. For more information about Wiley products, visit **www.wiley.com**

Library of Congress Cataloging-in-Publication Data
Wacksman, Barry, 1964-
  Connected by design : 7 principles of business transformation through functional integration / Barry Wacksman, Chris Stutzman. —First edition.
     1 online resource.
  Includes index.
  Description based on print version record and CIP data provided by publisher; resource not viewed.
  ISBN 978-1-118-90720-7 (pdf) —ISBN 978-1-118-90721-4 (epub) —ISBN 978-1-118-85820-2 (hardback)
  1. Strategic planning. 2. Management. 3. Marketing. I. Stutzman, Chris, 1972- II. Title.
  HD30.28
  658.4'012—dc23

2014009066

Printed in the United States of America

FIRST EDITION

HB Printing 10 9 8 7 6 5 4 3 2 1

To my muses, Alexandra and Alexander.
—Barry Wacksman

To Tara and Finn, my spark and my sunshine.
—Chris Stutzman

Contents

Connected
by Design

Introduction

They called it "The Day the World Stopped to Run."

On August 31, 2008, more than 750,000 people participated in the world's largest one-day running event, a 10K run called "the Nike+ Human Race." Ten thousand gathered to run the course on New York's tiny Randall's Island and then stayed on after for a rock concert. Tens of thousands more ran through the streets of Melbourne, Australia; along the Kallang River in Singapore; and out of Wembley Stadium in rainy London. Hundreds of other, smaller 10K events were organized that same day in cities and towns all around the globe. Runners logged more than four million miles in total and helped raise millions of dollars for cancer research, wildlife protection, and international refugee relief.[1]

Besides its grand and ambitious scale, the 2008 Nike+ Human Race owned another significant distinction. It was the first large-scale public athletic event to fully embrace the digital age. On the day of the race, runners equipped with Nike+ running shoe systems didn't need to travel to a major city in order to participate. Some never even left their homes. Once they signed up on the

Human Race website and paid the participation fee, they could run the 10K anywhere — on their favorite neighborhood routes or even on their home treadmills.

The $29 Nike+ iPod kit had been introduced in 2006. It was the first pedometer-like device that allowed runners to automatically record the time, distance, and pace of their runs. The kit comprises a tiny transmitter fitted into a Nike running shoe and a data receiver attached to an Apple iPod Nano. When the iPod is synced with a desktop computer, the running data is transferred to each runner's own registered Nike+ website.

During the 2008 Nike+ Human Race, runners from all over the world logged more than 800,000 miles through their Nike+ iPod kits. All their results were tabulated, ranked, and displayed on Nike's Human Race website. Tunisia was the fastest nation with an average run time of 41 minutes and 2 seconds. Rome, at 49 minutes, 21 seconds, was the fastest city. A U.S. runner with the Nike+ user name "Bibi017" recorded the fastest 10K time that day, at 33 minutes and 59 seconds.[2]

The data collected by Nike+ on a day-to-day basis provided its users with such helpful information that the Nike brand achieved a new level of relevance in their lives. One early fan of Nike+, a Maryland mom named Veronica Noone, said, "There's something about seeing what you've done, how your pace changes as you go up and down hills, that made me more motivated. I can log in to Nike+ and see what I've done over the past year. That's really powerful for me... The data is right there in white and green." She credited Nike with helping bring her postpregnancy weight down from 225 to 145 pounds.[3]

Throughout the 1980s and 1990s, Nike connected with consumers by relying on celebrity athlete endorsements and distinctive, groundbreaking advertising campaigns. For its 1987 ad promoting its Revolution line of shoes, Nike paid $500,000 for the rights to the Beatles' song "Revolution," marking the first time any Beatles recording had ever been used in a commercial.[4] The famous "Just Do It" tagline, widely acclaimed as one of the greatest in advertising history, was launched in 1988 and anchored Nike ads for the next 25 years. In 1990, Nike produced a memorable eight-page magazine ad with a "Just Do It" theme aimed at the women's running market. The ad contained a 377-word ode to female achievement, and when Oprah Winfrey read it aloud on her show, she was moved to tears.[5]

However, the unique connection that the Nike+ iPod kit created with its owners would spark a serious change in Nike's time-honored marketing practices. Nike's corporate leadership noticed that Nike+ members who checked in frequently to analyze their running data also bought a lot of Nike products online. The immediate result was an expanded U.S. market share for Nike running shoes following the Nike+ iPod launch. Through the first seven months of 2007, Nike captured 56.7 percent of the $3.6 billion U.S. running-shoe market, compared with 47.4 percent in 2006. As one market analyst noted, "No question, Nike Plus is one of the primary drivers of the company's running growth this year."[6] By the end of 2008, Nike's market share had climbed to 61 percent. Another analyst observed, "A significant amount of the growth comes from Nike+."[7]

Nike responded by pulling back on its TV spending. In 2006, an estimated 70 percent of the company's advertising dollars had been spent on TV ads alone. By the first half of 2007, Nike reduced the TV advertising share of its ad budget from 70 percent to just 45 percent.[8] With the Nike+ website drawing some of its most prized customers directly to Nike several times a week, reaching out to them through mass media no longer seemed so important. The company moved away from one-way advertising messages in general and invested in events like the Human Race and online offerings that would attract and involve Nike+ users.

There was also a marked change in Nike's direction as a brand and as a company. Stefan Olander (then Nike's director of digital content and now vice president of its Digital Sport division) stated that Nike+ iPod prompted Nike to reconsider its outlook on innovation. "In the past," Olander said, "the product was the end point of the consumer experience. Now it's the starting point."[9] By providing each Nike+ runner with a password-protected website of personalized running data, Nike had transformed ordinary Nike customers into active Nike+ *members*. Because of Nike+, the world's number-one athletic footwear and apparel company became something more than a seller of products. Nike+ called on Nike to become a social network provider and the digital home base to what is, in effect, the world's largest running club.

In the years that followed, Nike released a series of run-tracker devices designed to operate with the Nike+ platform. The Nike+ SportBand, released in 2008, was a wristband that removed the need for the iPod receiver attachment. The Nike+ SportWatch GPS, released in 2011, offered improved and advanced analytics for serious runners. Then the 2012 Nike+ FuelBand extended the product line to serve people who want to track their level of everyday physical activity at home and at work. FuelBand marked a considerable departure from the Nike image as a brand dedicated to serious exercise and athletic activity. That year, Nike+ was also released as a free app on the iPhone, so that anyone could join the Nike+ community and track his or her runs through the iPhone accelerometer and GPS without buying any Nike device at all.

In 2013, *Fast Company* magazine rated Nike the world's most innovative company, beating out all the famous tech titans of Silicon Valley.[10] The award marked a milestone in the transformation of Nike as a company. The world's largest seller of athletic apparel was now also a tech company with a wide range of digital products *and* services geared to help people in all kinds of athletic activities. As Olander told a packed house at the 2012 Cannes Lions advertising festival, "People now demand us not to say 'Just Do It.' They say 'Help me just do it. Enable me to do it.'"[11] Nike's marketers acknowledged as much in August 2013, when they celebrated the twenty-fifth anniversary of "Just Do It" by launching a campaign that claimed to take the tagline "from inspiration to action." The marketing campaign, dubbed Possibilities, provided Nike+ users with a series of running and activity challenges to be shared with millions of members belonging to "the Nike+ digital ecosystem."[12]

For decades, Nike had used only advertising images and messages to inspire athletic achievement. Introducing the Nike+ line of digital training tools enabled Nike to help athletes *attain* those achievements. Without fanfare, Nike moved from being a master of mass media consumer engagement to becoming an innovator in *digital consumer services*. In an era when many large companies have been humbled by challenges from disruptive start-up competitors, Nike was among the first large companies to grasp that "help me just do it, enable me to do it" is a rising consumer expectation, one that characterizes the digital age.

o A New Model for a New Century

The story of Nike's ongoing evolution as a company and a brand provides a vivid example of how digital technologies have redefined the nature of business growth and long-term success. Some of the world's most valuable and important companies — Amazon, Apple, and Google among them — have staked their futures on cultivating digital ecosystems of interrelated, interdependent products and services similar to the Nike+ platform and its related devices. Apple originated the ecosystem concept and remains its most successful practitioner. Nike learned from Apple through its Nike+ iPod partnership, and became the first traditional consumer products company to develop a substantial digital ecosystem of its own.

Each of these digital ecosystems is defined and supported by a distinctive online platform that functions as both a hub for the brand's digital services and as an invaluable portal to the brand's e-commerce offerings. These ecosystems succeed by nurturing ongoing relationships with the brand's most loyal customers. When such ecosystems are able to deliver consistent, valuable customer experiences, the brand's offerings become so distinctive, appealing, and compelling that brands in certain categories have attained positions of dominant and durable competitive advantage. Apple dominates sales of online music. Amazon dominates online shopping. Google dominates online search. Together, Apple and Google dominate the field of mobile operating systems.

The conception, design, and execution of such ecosystems represent a comprehensive new business model for the digital age. We call this business model *Functional Integration* because it relies on the interdependent dimensions of functionality and integration within ecosystems in order to deliver growth and profits. In line with Apple CEO Tim Cook's description of Apple's ecosystem as having both "breadth and depth,"[13] functionality describes the breadth of ecosystem elements and devices (iPhone, iPad, iMac), while integration describes the depth of that ecosystem's ability to integrate those elements in a user-friendly way (through Apple's iTunes store, App Store, and iCloud platform).

Growing a functionally integrated ecosystem requires continual innovation in each of these two dimensions. Adding or upgrading functional pieces provides new entry points for customers to join the ecosystem. Improving integration among the interdependent parts of the ecosystem sustains the interest and participation of those customers inside the ecosystem — and encourages them to buy still more functional pieces. "It's a fantastic business model," said Jay Campbell of Hart Research Associates in 2012. "The more [Apple] products you own, the more likely you are to buy more." Hart's research that year found that 55 million U.S. households owned at least one Apple device (including 61 percent of U.S. households with children) and that the average Apple household owned *three* Apple devices.[14]

The Apple ecosystem of devices and services exemplifies Functional Integration in its most fully realized form. As every Apple fanatic knows, a new piece of the Apple ecosystem allows you to unlock additional benefits from all the other pieces you may already own. A new Apple TV set-top box augments your iPhone's capabilities by mirroring the iPhone's videos and photos on the television screen through an integrated feature called AirPlay. A new iPad gains instant access to your computer's documents and browser bookmarks through the integrated iCloud. Music and videos purchased through Apple's iTunes store are instantly available for streaming to all your other Apple devices through iCloud, as well.

Each device and service that Apple offers is connected by design with all the others in multiple ways that reward customers for their increasingly deeper participation in the brand. Apple's ecosystem is aimed at drawing you in, making it ever more gratifying to buy Apple products and shun competitors, including devices that may offer lower prices and more attractive features. With its extremely limited product line, Apple has leveraged the strength of its ecosystem to achieve stratospheric heights of competitive advantage in the otherwise highly commoditized field of consumer electronics. Apple ended 2013 as the most valuable company on earth (in terms of market capitalization)[15] because investors recognize that Apple enjoys a unique and sustainable competitive advantage in a variety of categories. Most of Apple's rivals in smartphones, tablets, and personal computers are overmatched when pitting their stand-alone products against the overwhelming power of Apple's functionally integrated ecosystem.

Google's pursuit of Functional Integration, though not as rigorously disciplined as Apple's, may prove to have far greater reach in the long run. Growing outward from its online platform as the world's most powerful search engine, Google's functionally integrated ecosystem includes the Android mobile operating system, Apple's most formidable competitor. Google also owns the patents to Motorola's line of mobile phones and runs the Android-based Google Play app store. Other elements of the Google ecosystem include YouTube, Google Maps, Gmail, and dozens of other digital services. A team from our agency, R/GA, helped Google launch its Google Wallet electronic payment system in 2012 as yet another element, or node, in the Google ecosystem. The mobile app is functionally integrated in a wide variety of ways, allowing Gmail subscribers, for instance, to send cash to each other via simple email attachments. Google's long-term experiments with driverless cars, robots, and wearable technology (Google Glass) portend vast possibilities for Functional Integration that defy the imagination.

Amazon's approach to Functional Integration represents the broadest interpretation of Amazon's stated mission, to become the place where everyone "can find and discover anything they might want to buy online."[16] With the world's largest e-commerce site at the core of its ecosystem, Amazon has used it to branch out into the Kindle tablet and e-book reader, the Kindle app store, audiobooks, movie streaming, original video series production, cloud computing services, and door-to-door grocery delivery. Amazon's 2012 purchase of Audible digital audiobooks prompted development of one of the more creative examples of Functional Integration. Readers who buy both e-book and Audible versions of the same title can switch between the two without losing their places, thanks to an Amazon technology called Whispersync.

The prominence of the Amazon, Apple, and Google ecosystems may lead some to the mistaken conclusion that Functional Integration is an aspiration reserved for technology giants. Nothing could be further from the truth. We opened this Introduction with the story of Nike+ in order to underline how any kind of company—even a sports apparel company—can successfully deploy Functional Integration to create digital offerings that drive growth through consumer utility and customer retention.

A 2013 survey by Placed, a Seattle research firm, showed that the three retailers most threatened by Amazon's ecosystem are Bed, Bath and Beyond, Petsmart, and Toys R Us. Visitors at these retailers, the survey found, are among those most likely to inspect products in the store aisles and then go home and buy them at lower prices through Amazon.[17] Beyond competing head-to-head on price with Amazon, a difficult proposition, each of these retailers has a unique opportunity to use Functional Integration in order to gain back customer interest and secure customer retention. Each company serves a purpose of great importance to consumers—personal comfort, pet care, and child development. For each of them, a functionally integrated strategy that provides customer utility aligned with that retailer's purpose would offer new value in the shopping experience, value that Amazon could never duplicate.

Using Functional Integration in this way, to reimagine the creation of value for customers, is one of the seven fundamental principles we will discuss in the pages to come. Functional Integration calls on each company to reinterpret its mission and purpose in order to create new value propositions that respond to the ever-rising expectations of consumers in a digital, social, and mobile business environment.

Just as Nike's ecosystem has led to a reinterpretation of the company's role in athletic achievement, from apparel maker to digital training services provider, BMW is one of several leading carmakers that is using Functional Integration to reinterpret what it means to be in the auto industry. With the unveiling of its i3 electric vehicle in July 2013, BMW announced the development of a functionally integrated ecosystem of travel, mobility, and maintenance services.[18] And, as with all ecosystems, the BMW ecosystem is designed to accommodate partners in adjacent and related industry categories, including the car rental and lodging industries. Functionally integrated ecosystems that attract significant numbers of consumers are well positioned to open out into multisided industry platforms, generating new business-to-business revenues for the ecosystem host and all its partners.

o o o

Our agency, R/GA, was a part of the Nike+ development effort, and we maintain an internal team dedicated to continual innovation inside the Nike ecosystem. It was out of this close relationship that the term Functional Integration was coined. Our involvement in helping grow the Nike ecosystem required us to take part in all aspects of the work, including product conception, development, and design. It was a far cry from producing microsites, viral videos, and other traditional agency deliverables. The work with Nike was so different from our activities with all our other clients that we needed a new term to describe it. Barry Wacksman, R/GA's chief growth officer, developed the concept of Functional Integration in 2011, and it was introduced by R/GA that year at the 58th Cannes Lions International Festival of Creativity.

Since then, R/GA has continued to evolve as a digital agency, reinventing its business model to become a partner with its client companies in the process of helping them achieve Functional Integration. In 2012, R/GA brought on Chris Stutzman as its first managing director of business transformation and Jeff Mancini as its first vice president of product innovation. Chris is a veteran of Forrester Research, where he advised marketing executives on growing their brands through digital innovation. Jeff is a digital industry veteran who had formerly directed digital strategy at Interbrand.

Together, Chris and Jeff are R/GA's leaders and resident experts in the field of digital transformation consulting. They have assembled a team in the areas of business consulting, brand consulting, and innovation consulting to work alongside data analysts and strategists in communications insights, experience insights, and media/connections insights—forming what we call the "thinking" half of R/GA. These "thinkers" provide ideas and concepts to an even larger team of "makers"—designers, programmers, copywriters, project managers, and quality assurance testers—needed to build and manage the digital services and connected devices that bring Functional Integration to life.

R/GA has moved in this direction because we have seen, through our original research and client work, that Functional Integration is the emergent strategy of a new class of companies that are winning in the marketplace. Perpetual innovation and growth in mobile, social, and digital technologies all but guarantee that Functional Integration has become an essential business model for brands that want to keep up and give their customers new reasons to love them. We believe that industry-leading brands, in particular, need to pursue Functional Integration as a primary business model in order to retain precious brand equity and to remain relevant to their customers.

At the same time, we see how traditional strategies in advertising and marketing are losing traction with the public. In 2013, for the first time ever, the Interbrand 100 ranking of global brands placed two functionally integrated companies, Apple and Google, at the top of the list. Coca-Cola, which had held first place for fourteen years running, fell to third. In what might prove to be a watershed year for Functional Integration, three of the top five companies ranking highest in brand value growth were the three companies with model functionally integrated ecosystems: Apple, Google, and Amazon. Nike and BMW also saw double-digit growth in brand value that same year. Other perennially high-ranking brands, including Coke and Microsoft, were limited to growth in single digits.[19]

Such firms' traditional business model of creating products and then marketing them through mass advertising continues to fall in reliability, as the media environment fragments and loses its influence, especially among younger people. The Interbrand rankings provide evidence that Functional Integration represents a bulwark against this erosion of brand power at a time when product-by-product differentiation is proving more difficult than ever.

But the switch to Functional Integration is also difficult. Our experience has shown us the considerable cultural issues, obstacles, and pitfalls that every company faces in taking on the Functional Integration business model. Ecosystems require a depth of relationship with customers that few brands are prepared to accommodate. It also requires a depth of commitment on the company's part. Free digital tools such as Nike+, Gmail, and iTunes offer implied promises of a lifetime of cost-free support, and many of the functional and integrated additions to the ecosystem will not offer predictable streams of revenue or profits. (Apple, for instance, claims to run its App Store on a break-even basis.) Functional Integration has the power to transform your company, but only when it is engaged as a long-term play toward creating a sustainable competitive advantage.

o Structure of the Book

Every company follows a distinctive path toward Functional Integration, but we have found that certain principles apply to all who have proven to be most successful at it. We have organized the discussion of these seven principles in two parts. Part One of the book introduces you to Functional Integration as a business model and explores in the first three chapters its three fundamental underlying principles: delivering utility, engaging multiple contexts, and creating ecosystem synergies.

Part Two comprises four chapters that deal with the four essential principles for putting Functional Integration into action. Successful ecosystems are characterized by the distinctive ways in which they create, deliver, and capture value, and by supremely focused leadership that is willing to engage disruptive change within the organization. Implementing Functional Integration requires companies to reimagine how they create value for customers (in line with the first three principles of utility, multiple contexts, and synergy). Functional Integration then requires changes in how value is delivered. Above all, it requires redirecting the ecosystem toward capturing value for the company. Success in adhering to all three of these principles requires leadership that supports Functional Integration as the sole sustainable force for future growth of the company.

In the opening chapter, we tell the story of how McCormick, the U.S. market leader in flavors and spices, has taken the first crucial step toward Functional Integration by developing a digital service that reflects the principle of utility as a source of relevance. We describe how McCormick's FlavorPrint was created to provide daily utility for meal preparation, similar to the way Nike+ delivers daily utility for running. We show how McCormick uses Functional Integration strategies to combat store-brand competition, and in doing so, can leverage its consumer-facing FlavorPrint service to open up critical new business-to-business opportunities.

In Chapter Two, we dig deeper into the implications of doing business digitally by invoking the principle that context is king. Functional Integration allows brands to use new digital contexts to communicate with customers and deliver value to them in ways that advertising and marketing cannot. We explore in some detail how digital contexts such as search, participation, and visualization are superior forms of customer contact when compared with the traditional mass advertising context of "interruption." We look at carmakers, in particular, to show how an industry that was built on and that helped define the Golden Age of mainstream advertising has embraced the new digital reality of multiple contextual messages and services delivered through Functional Integration.

Chapter Three details the evolution of Functional Integration at Apple and Nike, demonstrating the principle that ecosystem synergy captures customers. We tell how Nike+ grew to become the functionally integrated focal point for all of Nike's major lines of business. We also relate some telling moments of inspiration and triumph, as well as some false starts and wrong assumptions, all of which have contributed to the ongoing transformation of Nike from apparel marketer to digital innovator.

Part Two, encompassing Chapters Four through Seven, demonstrates how to put the Functional Integration model to work. The fourth principle, in Chapter Four, is to reimagine how you create value. In order to conceive of new functionally integrated products and services, you must take a new look at the company's purpose and mission through three different lenses: the product lens, the brand lens, and the business lens. The product focus needs to move from incremental feature enhancement toward software innovation. The brand focus requires a departure from mass media messaging and the embrace of inventing tangible experiences and services for your customers. Ultimately, Functional Integration requires reimagining the future of your business in entirely new, transformative terms.

Chapter Five describes the ways in which Functional Integration requires you to redesign value delivery to your customers. We refer to the four areas of practical changes necessitated by this principle as the four Ts: territories, technology, talent, and teamwork. Reassessment of your competitive territories is important because in the digital age, disruptive competition can emerge from just about anywhere. Competing with potential disruptors, in turn, requires every company to make new kinds of technology choices. Talent and teamwork refer to the added staffing and new capabilities required by Functional Integration. People with new skills and abilities are needed to work on high-performance teams that operate outside and beyond typical marketing and technology roles and definitions.

Functional Integration success depends on attracting and retaining customers who are glad to pay premium prices for exceptional experiences within the ecosystem. Chapter Six discusses strategies for growing the breadth and depth of the functionally integrated ecosystem, based on the principle of growing the company's level of *captured* value. Thriving ecosystems require constant improvements in functionality (improving the value of the ecosystem) and integration (improving the overall ecosystem experience). Data and technologies are the tools for executing on both dimensions. Because ecosystems by nature generate a bounty of proprietary customer data, ecosystem managers must analyze this data and respond with innovative solutions in order to capture value and maintain a sustainable competitive advantage.

The final chapter emphasizes our belief in the principle that leadership in Functional Integration requires one to "lead like the world depends on it." Functional Integration represents nothing less than a revolution in how to understand, engage, and serve customers in the digital age. Functional Integration leaders such as Amazon, Apple, Google, and Nike are not only transforming their industries. They are transforming the world.

Winning this revolution goes back to the fundamental principles of providing customers with useful and meaningful digital services that help you manage the story of your brand in an authentic ongoing dialogue. Product innovation is the starting point for all such meaningful dialogues. We will stress throughout the coming pages how fresh opportunities for innovation must be identified and acted on quickly in order to sustain your relevance with customers. Those opportunities must also be tested and analyzed to show that they can generate e-commerce growth while delivering value to customers.

Consumer research, in turn, should be directed toward finding new brand strategies that connect the pieces of the ecosystem around the company's core mission or ambition, whether it is "to enhance athletic performance" at Nike or "to organize the world's knowledge" at Google. With the stories of these and other leaders in Functional Integration, we will show how, time and again, the greater the ambition and the more vivid the mission, the greater the chances of success.

Most companies, however, are woefully unprepared to evolve in this new direction. Amazon, Apple, Google, and Nike are all commonly lauded as admirable companies. But their Functional Integration business models make them outliers, to say the least, among most consumer product companies found in the Fortune 500. Mature firms tend to be organized as product marketers with portfolios of brands to promote. They go to market on an item-by-item basis and squeeze out growth through mass media advertising. For decades they have relied on the dual strategies of horizontal and vertical integration to expand their markets and control internal costs.

However, most of our agency's clients tell us that these strategies for growth through horizontal and vertical integration no longer deliver the same kinds of results that they did in the past. In the mature markets of the United States and Western Europe, low single-digit growth for major companies is common. The media engine that fueled brand growth for decades is no longer able to aggregate the same audiences in the same way as in the past. Even though more people are watching more television than ever, the fragmentation of networks combined with the rise of time-shifting and commercial skipping have taken a huge bite out of the power of television ads to deliver sales results.

The other problem is that horizontal integration has sown the seeds of its own destruction. It has created a marketplace so crowded that no single brand has any chance to gain leverage with consumers. The pace of new product introductions has exploded. In 1992, approximately 10,000 food and beverage items and 6,000 nonfood grocery items were introduced into supermarkets for the first time. Less than 20 years later, in 2010, that number had grown to 20,000 new food and beverage items and 25,000 new nonfood items.[20] These are just introductions of new products—all piled on top of tens of thousands of existing products.

Clayton Christensen, author of *The Innovator's Solution*, famously noted that "making highly differentiable products with strong cost advantages is a license to print money."[21] High differentiation, however, is difficult to achieve in today's crowded marketplace. Strong cost advantages are just as hard to come by in a world of inexpensive imports and other downward forces on prices. The inadequacy of horizontal and vertical integration to produce high differentiation and strong cost advantages partly explains why most of the companies "printing money" on Christensen's terms are the ones that rely on Functional Integration.

Our point is not that horizontal and vertical integration are obsolete strategies. The need for new product introductions and supply chain efficiencies will never go away. Our point is that these two essential business strategies are no longer reliable sources of sustainable competitive advantage.

One way to look at Functional Integration is to consider it as a higher evolution of both horizontal and vertical integration, adapted to the contexts of the digital age. Apple provides the perfect example. As with most horizontally integrated companies, Apple's product lines seek to appeal to different consumer niches by offering products with varying features at varying price points. But Apple's product lines are very small compared with those of its competitors. For instance, Apple makes only several models of the iPhone. The strategy is to offer a very limited number of highly appealing entry points into the Apple ecosystem. By contrast, other mobile phone manufacturers that lack such ecosystems need to put out much longer lines of mobile phones with various features at various price points in order to compete on a product-by-product basis in a wide range of niches—the classic horizontal strategy.

Apple's choice to limit its lines of products yields direct cost savings in supply chain management and other efficiencies of vertical integration. A smaller number of models results in greater efficiencies of scale in manufacturing, which in turn create more negotiating power over suppliers. Fewer models also mean lower development costs. Apple was named *Businessweek*'s most innovative company every year from 2005 to 2011, but its relatively small product line helped keep R&D costs at only 2.7 percent of revenues, less than half the 6.5 percent R&D costs incurred at the Blackberry's parent company, RIM. Smaller lines of products even help reduce overhead. Apple's SGA (sales, general, and administrative costs) were found on a five-year average to be just 8.8 percent, compared with 22 percent at Sony and IBM, and 12.4 percent at Dell.

British business professor Loizos Heracleous made note of the aforementioned comparisons in a 2013 study of Apple's strategy, writing that Apple has defied conventional thinking, which states that "a company competing on innovation, outstanding design or service excellence will not be able to reach intense levels of efficiency, since these capabilities are costly to develop and maintain."[22] Heracleous pointed to economist Michael Porter's popular assertion that a firm can choose to compete either through differentiation or through cost control, but not through both.

Porter, for decades one of the business world's most influential theorists, has said in essence that a company's lead strategy must be either vertical (cost leadership) or horizontal (differentiation through niche strategies or innovation).

Thanks to Functional Integration, Apple has defied Porter's theory. Functional Integration doesn't require push-pull tensions between vertical cost savings and horizontal differentiation. What Porter could not have foreseen is how the digital ecosystem of the Functional Integration business model can reduce costs *through* high differentiation and innovation. The synergies created within well-designed digital ecosystems enable the accretion of value on an exponential basis for customers and companies alike. Amazon, Apple, and Google rank among the most admired companies on earth as a result.

We believe that companies that fail to use Functional Integration as a business model will discover soon enough that both growth and profits will be elusive in the future. That's because everything that was true about Functional Integration in 2013 will be truer in 2018 or 2025. The media landscape will continue to fragment, and advertising's ability to drive sales will continue to weaken. Commoditization will continue to grow in strength. Customer expectations will grow inexorably for brand experiences that are personalized, customized, localized, interactive, useful, informative, and entertaining (the contexts of the digital age). The digital technologies required to deliver on all of the expectations will continue to disrupt existing business models, sometimes in ways that are utterly unpredictable.

In May 2013, a McKinsey Global Institute report projected that industries with combined annual operating costs of $36 *trillion* face imminent technological disruption by the so-called Internet of Things—tiny sensors and actuators embedded in machines and products. McKinsey estimated that such microsensors had dropped in price by 80 to 90 percent since 2008, and that there had been a 300 percent rate of growth in applications of these technologies as a result.[23]

Which companies do you think will be best positioned to innovate, to create value, and to capture value when common household products can be shipped with tiny inexpensive sensors embedded in them? Nike or Adidas? Apple or Sony? Google or Yahoo? Amazon or Walmart? The same question might be asked about other disruptive technologies that McKinsey cited in the same report, including advanced robotics, automated knowledge work, and 3-D printing. The answer is the same for each disruptive technology. Companies with functionally integrated digital ecosystems will be poised to profit from technological disruption, while other companies will suffer.

From that perspective, we are not overstating the case when we say that any delay in engaging a Functional Integration approach for your company may prove costly and possibly fatal. Consider how Philips, the one-time consumer electronics giant in the days of CDs and DVDs, decided to leave the industry entirely in 2013, surrendering the field to Apple's ecosystem.[24] Sony's electronics division, which lost a cumulative $8.5 billion between 2003 and 2013, stands to be Apple's next victim.[25]

Functional Integration, as you will see, is so effective at creating and capturing value for those who do it right, that every day you neglect to use Functional Integration to win, you risk growing one day closer to losing out to those who are.

Part One
The Model

1

The Growth Challenge of the 21st Century

Principle One: Utility is relevance.

The U.S. consumer's appetite for spicier food has been on a steady upswing at least since 2004, according to some industry reports. Between 2004 and 2009 alone, sales of spices and seasonings grew by 30 percent.[1] Younger generations in particular are expected to sustain an increasing preference for spicier, more adventurous cooking and dining. A 2012 report by *Food Technology* magazine showed that in the previous two years, the preference for spicy foods had grown 9 percent among Americans ages 25 to 34 and 13 percent among those ages 35 to 44.[2]

All these trends should register as great news for Maryland-based McCormick and Company. McCormick's brands occupy more than 45 percent of the U.S. spice and seasoning market, dwarfing its nearest competitors, and it dominates the category in grocery stores and supermarkets throughout the country.

There remains plenty of room for growth in the size of the overall market, too, as surveys say that fully half of all the steak and chicken cooked in U.S. kitchens is seasoned with only salt and pepper or with no seasoning at all.[3]

Other trends, however, pose some challenges for McCormick's future domestic sales. Since the 2009 recession, consumers have become more price conscious and less brand loyal than ever before. The rising desire for spicy foods might not benefit McCormick at all if penny-pinching consumers prefer to fill their pantries with cheaper spices sold under generic and store-brand labels.

Competition from bargain-priced store brands is a problem for all the top U.S. food brands, from Campbell's to Skippy. In order to preserve market share, most major brands rely on coupons, temporary price reductions, and all sorts of marketing promotions to persuade consumers to pay a little more for superior taste and quality. But McCormick faces a peculiar obstacle in this regard. For most food brands, it is only one simple step from purchase to consumption, so the primary message of most food marketing is very simple. It tries to inspire the consumer to buy the product.

The consumer's relationship with spices and seasonings, by contrast, is fairly indirect. Spices are not impulse buys, like bottles of soda or packs of chewing gum. McCormick marketers, before they have any chance of inspiring you to buy the product, need to inspire you to *prepare a meal*. The enjoyment of McCormick products requires a whole series of preliminary steps — deciding to cook, choosing a recipe, assembling ingredients. This is the "flavor lifecycle," as it's called within McCormick. A recipe or a meal idea that is promoted by McCormick begins the cycle. Next you need to follow through with planning the meal and putting McCormick products on your shopping list. Then there's the shopping trip and subsequent meal preparation — all necessary stages in the cycle before you and your family can finally enjoy the flavor of some new or different product from McCormick.

Because of the flavor lifecycle, McCormick marketing materials have typically highlighted simple recipes accompanied by vivid images of mouth-watering meals. The distribution and promotion of recipes is such an essential element of McCormick marketing that the company relies on a sophisticated sensory and culinary team in suburban Baltimore to generate new recipes to accommodate the evolving American palate. Information-rich marketing of this kind is ideal for the digital age, and McCormick has aggressively shifted its marketing mix accordingly. McCormick's social network hub for backyard barbequers, the Grillerhood, has drawn more than one million fans to its Facebook page. Digital marketing, which had consumed just 4 percent of the company's marketing budget in 2010, tripled its budget share to 12 percent in 2012.[4]

Now that McCormick recipes and their accompanying promotions are easier than ever before to distribute through social media, McCormick faces a new problem characteristic of the digital age: how to be heard above all the noise. The Internet is exploding with recipes, including those contributed by major cookbook publishers, cooking magazine websites, celebrity chefs, and cable TV channels. The number-one recipe website, Allrecipes.com, is one of the top 50 sites in U.S. Internet traffic, with 30 million unique visitors per month.[5] The website claims to offer more than one million recipes, which amounts to more than 40 lifetimes' worth of meals.

Whenever you face a bewildering number of choices—or even a half-dozen choices—the natural questions that arise are, "Which of these choices are any good?" and "Which one would I like best?" Recipe sites are cluttered with "thumbs-up" recommendations and special lists of "Top Recipes" and "Most Popular Recipes" and "Top 10 Searches." But popularity rankings and recommendations from anonymous strangers aren't always reliable in matters of personal taste. And even if you were to trust all those lists and recommendations, how then do you choose from among a half-dozen highly recommended, five-star-rated recipes, each supported by scores of glowing reviews and hundreds of raised thumbs?

A digital tool might offer a solution. Internet giants Amazon and Netflix have come to dominate their respective categories in books and movies by developing recommendation engines that offer their members suggested selections tailored to their members' individual tastes. By analyzing your purchase history, the algorithmic formulas that drive these recommendation engines can predict your preferences with a very high degree of certainty. If McCormick could develop a similarly personalized search resource for recipes, the company would have an invaluable tool for differentiating its recipes from those of all the other recipe sites. The company might also become something more than just another food brand in the minds of its customers. McCormick could be known as the Amazon of recipes, the Netflix of flavor.

○ Your FlavorPrint, Like Your Fingerprint

Every successful Functional Integration effort has daily utility as a core objective. Nike provides daily utility for its 21 million Nike+ members through its ecosystem of running devices and services. It's no coincidence that the three most fully functionally integrated companies—Amazon, Apple, and Google—are all makers of mobile devices, because mobile devices are a vital medium for providing daily utility within each of their respective ecosystems.

Functionally integrated ecosystems develop strong customer followings because they offer digital services that are useful and meaningful in their user's everyday lives. Services such as iTunes and Nike+ provide personalized customizable tools that provide users with direct, tangible benefits. Functional Integration drives long-term profitability only to the extent that it enables companies to build long-term relationships by offering such tools as entry points to their ecosystems.

A functionally integrated digital service is emphatically *not* a marketing campaign. Interactive marketing is more likely to offer entertainment, discussion, special offers, and little else. Although such efforts may succeed in achieving short-term purposes as marketing tools, they lack the essential utility, long-term vision, and commitment that exemplify functionally integrated digital services.

We began this chapter with the example of McCormick in order to show how a successful horizontally integrated company can draw on that success in taking the first important step down the path to Functional Integration. The simplicity and focus of McCormick's development of a digital recipe search tool is notable because in many respects, it resembles the first such efforts by all the big players in Functional Integration.

Apple's iTunes began in 2001 as an attractive, unpretentious library for organizing your personal collection of digital music. It didn't make any money for Apple when it launched because Apple didn't begin selling digital music through iTunes until 2003. Nike+ had a similar start as a free website that allowed runners to manually record their daily runs. Google began as nothing more than the most useful and reliable search tool on the web. Amazon started out as a user-friendly online bookseller.

Each of these fairly modest and free digital offerings provided handy, reliable tools that expressed the authentic relevance of the brand to each customer in highly personal ways. It was this specific quality of relevance through utility that set each company on its own particular course toward what are now very profitable functionally integrated ecosystems of digital products and services.

For McCormick to move in this direction of daily utility, it was important to take stock of the company's unique position in the food industry. Beyond the spices and seasonings sold with the McCormick label, McCormick and Company makes and distributes products under dozens of brand names around the world, including Lawry's, Zatarain's, Kamis, Schwartz, and Ducros. McCormick is also a global leader in providing flavoring products to fast-food companies, foodservice businesses, and other food industry members. CEO Alan Wilson once told analysts, "we believe no matter where or what you eat each day, you're likely to enjoy something that's flavored by McCormick."[6] As a result, within McCormick and Company there is a depth of knowledge about the sensory science of flavors that ranks second to none.

Deep expertise of this kind can be an invaluable asset when it comes to developing Functional Integration strategies. Back in 2004, researchers at Nike with a sophisticated grasp of the science of running were crucial to the successful development of Nike+. They were aware of studies establishing a relationship between running speed and the measure of milliseconds that the runner's foot remains on the ground in midstride. That insight, and the science related to it, led to the development of the Nike+ iPod shoe sensor.

McCormick's staff has food science capabilities just as impressive as the running science capabilities inside Nike. How could McCormick use a small fraction of that knowledge to develop a personalized tool that would make McCormick an indispensable resource for anyone in search of the perfect recipe?

When McCormick and R/GA began to work together on this question, it was necessary to appreciate that most consumers understand very little about flavor. We all love tasty foods, of course, but the vast majority of us lack the vocabulary to describe the tastes we enjoy most. So when we seek out a recipe or select an entrée in a restaurant, we're more likely to sort our choices according to the main ingredient. "I think I'll make chicken tonight," or "The salmon special sounds good." Then we hope we'll enjoy the flavor when the chicken is done or the salmon arrives.

Flavors remain a mystery to most of us because our sense of taste is a very complex matter. Sugar is sweet and lemons are sour, but what is a tomato? The flavor of each tomato is a delicate balance of sugar, acid, and about 400 volatile aromatic chemicals, only a dozen of which are detectable by the human nose.[7] Put a tomato in a stew with chicken, carrots, celery, onion, and a half-dozen spices, and how would you describe the dish? You'd say it's chicken stew. You'd identify it by its main ingredient, because its unique flavor, distinct from hundreds of other chicken stew recipes, defies your description.

McCormick knows from its consumer research that our lack of knowledge about our own palates tends to get us stuck in "food ruts." We become familiar with a few dishes we know we like, and we stay with them. A busy mom with a family of picky eaters is relieved when she can identify a handful of reliable dishes that everyone likes. Those dishes become her go-to recipes for peace and harmony at the dinner table. Why take a chance on some great-looking new recipe you discovered today online? The recipe might have earned a hundred recommendations, but if the kids don't like it, you'll just end up having to cook twice that night.

But what if you knew enough about your flavor preferences (or the preferences of the family's pickiest eater) that you could identify a new and different recipe that promised a 95 percent chance of success? With the risk of failure reduced, you might be tempted to try something that looks a little strange or exotic, perhaps even a dish you always assumed you wouldn't like. That's the goal of the McCormick digital service called FlavorPrint.

Similar to your fingerprint, your FlavorPrint is your unique identifying marker. It is a handy profile of the flavors you like best and the ones you'd rather avoid. When matched in an automated search with recipes on McCormick's various websites, Flavor-Print gives you more than just new ideas. Its recommendations give you the confidence that taking a risk on a new recipe will be rewarded. FlavorPrint is a tool for easing you out of your food rut.

To begin the FlavorPrint project, McCormick and R/GA personnel needed to examine McCormick's vast storehouse of flavor knowledge and decide how much of it would be relevant to the everyday cook. Food scientists will tell you that we can sense over 3,000 different flavors, but that number is far too unwieldy for the kind of database that would drive the FlavorPrint recommendation engine. So McCormick's experts were able to develop for FlavorPrint a more manageable flavor portfolio of 33 primary, determinative flavors. Your range of preferences on the basis of these 33 flavors is what gives you your unique FlavorPrint. They include some of the basic tastes, such as salty, sweet, and bitter, along with more subtle flavors: floral, herby, woody, and licorice.

Although FlavorPrint's conception had been inspired by the examples of Amazon and Netflix, the actual underlying architecture of those two recommendation engines isn't useful at all in determining food preferences. Amazon and Netflix rely on a computer data technique known as "collaborative filtering." In a kind of "birds of a feather" sorting process, Amazon and Netflix match your choice patterns with those of members with similar patterns in order to deduce what other books and movies you will probably like. But the food-tasting aesthetic does not lend itself to the collaborative filtering process. The fact that two people share a love of both tomatoes and licorice, for instance, will not help you predict their mutual like or dislike of a dish heavily flavored with cilantro.

So instead the FlavorPrint team pursued a process similar to that of the Music Genome Project, the type of digital engine that powers the music site Pandora. Pandora develops playlists for its various channels (named after prominent artists ranging from Bob Dylan to Lady Gaga) by analyzing songs in a way that breaks down each track into its component parts—rhythm, timbre, dynamic range, and more than 300 other criteria. Then, songs that match the distinct digital fingerprint closest to that of, say, Lady Gaga's music, would be assigned to play on the Lady Gaga channel. Rather than use the more common music genre labels (which involve fairly crude and subjective judgments, akin to grouping recipes according to their main ingredients), this kind of computer analysis assesses how the various elements of music interact to create a song's distinctive sonic effect. It turns out that the mélange of sounds that make up a piece of recorded music is not so different from the mélange of flavors that produce a delicious and satisfying dish.

An optometry exam determines your eyeglass prescription after you've looked through a set series of lenses and given feedback on your view through each lens. FlavorPrint determines your flavor profile through a similar process. After you register with FlavorPrint, the website displays a series of food items and prompts you to give each one a thumbs-up or thumbs-down. The process takes about three minutes, after which you receive a FlavorPrint assessment of your three favorite defining flavors, which might be, for example, Tomatoey, Herby, and Garlic Onionish. A graphic plots all 33 possible flavors as spokes on a color wheel, with each spoke sized to reflect your level of preference for that flavor.

After that, the FlavorPrint page offers you a set of recipes especially matched to your FlavorPrint profile. An analysis of recipe ingredients allows each recipe to be similarly FlavorPrinted with a color wheel of its own, so you can tell at a glance how each recipe's featured flavors match your own preferences. The recipe is also accompanied by FlavorPrint's algorithmic reliability estimations, expressed as percentages. Then, if you want to take a little more time to make your FlavorPrint more accurate, you can click through to be quizzed on dozens of additional food and cooking preferences. The more you tell FlavorPrint about yourself, the more accurately it will predict your flavor preferences and the recipes most likely to satisfy them.

There is nothing else quite like FlavorPrint in the digital world of recipes. Launched in beta stage in early 2013, FlavorPrint as a personalized recommendation engine has the potential to provide McCormick with a distinct competitive advantage over all other recipe sites, an advantage as formidable, perhaps, as the advantage Netflix enjoyed while conquering the video rental industry.

Netflix's movie streaming service is so popular that one 2012 study showed it accounts for one-third of all downstream Internet traffic in North America between 9 a.m. and midnight.[8] Netflix's own data reveals that 75 percent of all that traffic is initiated through recommendations from its personalization algorithms.[9] Similarly, FlavorPrint's automated recommendation can end up saving users time and needless worry combing general recipe sites, while surprising them with recipes they may never have dreamed they would like.

○ Technology as Business Transformation

The 2012 announcement of FlavorPrint as a McCormick initiative attracted some attention for the company from the food industry trade media.[10] FlavorPrint also won several design and agency awards for its utility and user experience.[11] As a handy tool that can help develop the taste palate of anyone using it, FlavorPrint is good for McCormick's bottom line because, as the market leader in spices and seasonings, McCormick stands to win whenever consumers start making more flavorful choices. Some spice sales inspired by FlavorPrint might also be captured by McCormick's competitors, but many of the dishes in the McCormick recipe database call for the use of McCormick's proprietary blends and other branded products (Lawry's blends, Grill Mates marinades) for which there are few substitutes.

The reason for developing FlavorPrint, however, is not to sell a few more McCormick products in the short term.

By offering a highly personalized service that outshines the predictive capabilities of all other online recipe sites, FlavorPrint has positioned McCormick to become a uniquely trusted and indispensable partner to the home cook, and to all the related companies and industries with a stake in home cooking.

The speed of technological change makes it difficult to guess at how exactly FlavorPrint will achieve this status. On the day of FlavorPrint's beta launch in 2013, the technologies that might determine its success 5 or 10 years later had probably not yet been invented. This is true with nearly every service offered as the starting point of a functionally integrated ecosystem. When Amazon was founded as an online bookseller in 1995, who would have supposed that the company would use its platform to become the world's largest publisher of e-books? Did anyone at Apple foresee, on the launch of iTunes in 2001, that by 2009, iTunes members would be buying movies to watch on their *iPhones*?

The brief history of Functional Integration tells us that the business model works best when its long-term goal is to achieve inelasticity for its brand, when the digital ecosystem of products and services can stake a claim of "ownership" to a certain market space. The smart move for McCormick would be to build out its FlavorPrint ecosystem with the aim of dominating "flavor" in the minds of consumers, no different from the way Amazon dominates books, Google dominates search, and Apple's iTunes dominates digital music.

If this seems like an unrealistic objective, consider that never before in the history of marketing has it been possible to engage consumers both on this highly personal level and on this wide, mass scale. Functionally integrated ecosystems like Apple's and Google's are embedded in everyday life with a reach and frequency formerly associated only with paid advertising. From such a digital platform, anything is possible, as Apple and Google have shown.

While FlavorPrint was still in its beta stages, McCormick executives began exploring opportunities to provide FlavorPrint as a recipe recommendation engine for online grocery shopping sites. "Retailers are focused on developing the in-store experience, but they want to figure out how to take that one-to-one relationship into the digital space," said Andrew Foust, McCormick's director of digital business development. "FlavorPrint offers a personalized solution that our retailers have been overwhelmingly supportive of, and they are excited to work with us as we move forward beyond the beta test."[12]

Partnerships of this kind would enroll larger numbers of FlavorPrint members than McCormick could ever manage on its own. From there, FlavorPrint might achieve enough traction to become an attractive feature for restaurant chains, online recipe sites, and packaged food producers. In some instances, licensing FlavorPrint within the food industry might begin to earn McCormick new streams of revenue.

All of these potential partnerships would serve as new sources of FlavorPrint enrollments, providing McCormick with precious consumer data that could be used to refine FlavorPrint's services even further. A credible long-term goal for FlavorPrint is to become the source of multiple revenue streams for McCormick, from licensing, consulting, and the sale of any number of business-to-business products. In the process, McCormick will have transformed its business model from that of a 20th-century market leader in spices and seasonings to a 21st-century standard-bearer of flavor.

The likelihood of any of this happening for McCormick rests on the question of whether FlavorPrint can provide a compelling and reliable level of utility to its users. Thanks to the power of social and mobile technologies, the ability to build strong ongoing relationships with consumers through digital utility will likely determine which companies can dominate their consumer categories in the years to come. Apple, Amazon, and Google have already managed to cement their status as market leaders in this way, through their ecosystems' utility, attractiveness, and marketing power.

Functional Integration can provide this sharp competitive edge because it is based on transformative digital technologies, and transformative technologies have always caused massive disruption in consumer markets. The Internet, social media, and mobile communications have produced enormous changes in the way consumers relate to the companies they buy from. Companies that fail to maximize the potential of these technologies will either fail or end up as undifferentiated, commoditized also-rans. A look at the past suggests that this has always been so. The history of business is the history of winners edging out losers by adapting to technological change.

Many of the most revered brands names of today had their beginnings in the 1880s, when the spread of railroads across the U.S. landscape first enabled companies to access markets on a national scale. Names such as Heinz, Coca-Cola, Levi's, Procter & Gamble, and many others, McCormick included, were founded during this time, along with many thousands of others who are lost to history.

Over the decades, countless companies were either bankrupted or gobbled up by larger companies in the drive for economies of scale, the process known as horizontal integration. To grow in the industrial age required the constant expansion into new products and brands, enlarging the portfolio and inventing new things that the consuming public desires. This strategy is so commonplace that most of us rarely even give it a thought. Company leaders have long understood that you always risk erosion in your market share unless you continue along the route of line extensions, segmentation, and exploiting brand equity to serve more customers and fill consumer niches in adjacent categories or subcategories.

Coca-Cola was once a famously stubborn holdout in this regard. From the Great Depression through the 1950s, Coke's dominance of the soft drink market was so strong that in many Southern states, the word "coke" is still used to refer to *any* soft drink, just as facial tissues are called Kleenexes. For decades, the iconic Coca-Cola brand sold only the single soft drink formula, and until the late 1950s, that single formula was available only in one size, the 10-ounce distinctively shaped bottle. When Coke introduced a diet cola in 1963, it was called Tab, not Diet Coke. Coke was, in the words of one historian, "the most changeless of America's consumer goods."[13]

Pepsi was Coca-Cola's long-suffering rival for many years. Pepsi tried and failed to compete with Coke on price and on bottle sizes, all to little or no avail. Then a new management group at Pepsi hit on horizontal integration in the 1960s. PepsiCo offered Pepsi Light and Diet Pepsi to undercut Coca-Cola's position and start eating away at Coca-Cola's enormous market share. By 1983, Pepsi was outselling Coca-Cola head-to-head in supermarkets. Coca-Cola's market share was eroding, as it was saddled with a single-product strategy that couldn't compete with Pepsi's horizontal challenge.[14]

Finally in 1982, Coca-Cola broke with tradition and introduced Diet Coke. After that came Caffeine-Free Coke, Cherry Coke, and Caffeine-Free Diet Coke. Then came Coke Zero, a version of diet soda specifically developed to be marketed to men who wanted a calorie-free soft drink but didn't want to be seen buying a product with the word "diet" on it. Coke Zero was followed by Vanilla Coke Zero and Cherry Coke Zero. The Coca-Cola Company became a global master of horizontal integration. Its beverage brands alone literally run the gamut from A to Z, and include Aquapure, Bacardi Mixers, Barq's, Full Throttle, Fuze Tea, Evian, Fanta, Fresca, Fruitopia, glacéau vitaminwater, Honest Tea, Inca Kola, Master Pour, Mello Yello, Minute Maid, Monster,

Odwalla, Pibb Zero, Powerade, Sprite, Worx Energy, and Zico coconut water.[15] Coke ended up winning the cola wars in the process. Coca-Cola remains by far the number-one soft drink in the U.S. market, with Diet Coke running second and Pepsi-Cola an also-ran third.[16]

Horizontal integration was sparked in its earliest days by the spread of the railroads. Vertical integration was powered by the spread of computers. During the final quarter of the 20th century, the nascent information technology industry drove a trend toward cost cutting and efficiency. Automated information technologies provided new levels of revelatory data that allowed far more cost-effective allocations of resources within each company's vertical supply chain. For the first time ever, executives could see where profits were being sacrificed, and could take steps to staunch the bleeding.

Every single Fortune 500 corporation went through company-wide implementations of enterprise resource planning (ERP) tools from software leaders like SAP and others. Consulting firms including IBM, Accenture, and EDS provided the professional expertise required to get these systems up and running. Tighter control of the supply chain became the best and quickest way to squeeze profits, as did the replacement of human workers with automated processes and machine controls. Companies looked to cut costs at every stage of production. As companies became more horizontally integrated to drive top-line growth, they simultaneously became more vertically integrated to drive bottom-line cost savings and boost profitability. Until the rise of Functional Integration, these two dimensions of horizontal and vertical integration directed most if not all of corporate competitive strategy.

Relentless horizontal expansion, in particular, is responsible for the bloated marketplace of the 21st century. Consumers have a dizzying array of choices in nearly every mature category, more choices than at any time in human history. The result is that almost every industry operates in a consumer market that has never been so elastic. This is the growth challenge of the 21st century for most, but not all, firms. It is no coincidence that the rare exceptions in which consumer choice remains remarkably *inelastic* can be found among digital companies dependent on Functional Integration — Apple, Google, and Amazon.

Horizontal integration can still produce profits if your company manages to play the game a little bit better than your competitors. Every now and then, a hit product or brand manages to break out a new category, the way Unilever's Axe created the body spray as a complement to the highly commoditized category of deodorants and antiperspirants. Or an entrepreneur comes along with a market hit like Snapple, which is then bought by one of the Fortune 500. Hoping for hits, however, is not a corporate strategy.

In 2010, major national brands received a scare that demonstrated the fragile grip they maintain on their markets. That year, Walmart started dropping some of the biggest brand names from its shelves. Walmart's aim was to reduce the number of items it had to track and inventory, but it was also to make more room in its stores for its own Great Value store-brand items. Prior to 2010, Walmart carried four different brands of plastic storage bags: Glad, Hefty, Ziploc, and Great Value. Suddenly, Glad and Hefty were gone from its shelves.[17]

"For many commodity-like products, second best has proven good enough," wrote John Jannarone, the *Wall Street Journal's* "Heard on the Street" columnist.

Walmart discovered, however, that when some shoppers can't find their preferred brands at Walmart, they shop somewhere else. Walmart sales slumped and in response, the company reversed course and brought back 8,500 brand-name products in a 2011 promotion called "It's Back."[18]

The message was clear, though. The retailers on which all consumer brands rely have strong incentives to promote private-label products instead, because private labels tend to earn retailers higher gross margins and greater customer loyalty.[19] Meanwhile, the increasing availability of private-label alternatives will continue to foster the notion in some consumers' minds that this branded detergent or that branded snack food isn't significantly better than the store's own product.

Functional Integration in its most fundamental form can serve as a hedge against this trend toward commoditization because it has the power to drive consumer preference and gain market share. If you are unable to establish an authentic brand relationship by giving your customers something relevant to their daily lives, the only difference they will see between your brand and Walmart's Great Value is the price difference. They will opt for those cheaper options, or—as in the case of Walmart and its removal of Glad Bags—your retail channels will make the decision for you, eliminating your products from the shelves and eliminating them from your customer's attention in the process.

o Owning the Space

When McCormick studies the consumers who respond to its digital marketing efforts, company officials like what they see. Visitors to the McCormick website and social channels spend upwards of 40 percent more on McCormick products than the average McCormick customer. The digital consumer, says CEO Wilson, "is a very engaged consumer, and is one we're increasingly reaching out to."[20]

FlavorPrint was first unveiled as a McCormick initiative during a 2012 investor conference, when Ken Stickevers, president of McCormick's U.S. consumer products division, hailed it as "a breakthrough application of technology" and compared its appeal to that of Amazon's recommendation engine.

Gaining greater exposure for FlavorPrint through partnership channels will be critical to FlavorPrint's success because Functional Integration platforms tend to be "sticky" in marketing terms. People who sign up for digital services tend to use them, and then they develop loyalty to the brand behind them. The challenge is to attract large numbers of consumers to the Flavor-Print platform and its features. Without effective strategies to give customers the chance to "stick," some excellent digital platforms sit underutilized, like expensive sports cars that never leave the garage.

Personalization is a key to stickiness because one of the key attractions of functionally integrated services is that these services help people know themselves better. We helped another R/GA client, L'Oreal Paris, launch My Signature Beauty in January 2013 as a way of offering each visitor a customized assessment of her hair care and cosmetic needs. Similar to FlavorPrint, My Signature Beauty makes recommendations that are dependent on the customer's willingness to share personal information. Visitors are asked to input their hair color, eye color, and skin condition, and the nature of the beauty results they seek, whether it's to repair damaged hair or remedy dry skin. An algorithmic recommendation engine sorts through thousands of products in 15 different L'Oreal sub-brands to provide a comprehensive, personalized report.

By giving McCormick and L'Oreal a highly detailed profile of yourself, you offer these companies enough information to send you special offers designed to appeal to your particular profile. Most company email blasts send you offers for what they want to sell you. When you sign up for weekly emails through functionally integrated services from McCormick or L'Oreal Paris, you're alerted mainly to products that those companies know you'll be interested in.

The other aspect of this two-way information flow is that McCormick and L'Oreal are learning more about their customer bases. When you follow the FlavorPrint prompts and respond fully to the digital questionnaire, you give McCormick a full picture of how many of their close customers bake, how many poach, how many own a blender, and how many own a juicer. All that knowledge about its best, most loyal customers will inevitably affect McCormick's product mix and product development decisions.

So even if few readers are aware of FlavorPrint or My Signature Beauty on reading this chapter, that's hardly an indication of the potential those digital services represent. Functional Integration, dependent as it is on gaining new memberships, grows in strength according to the snowball effect. Amazon, Apple, and Google launched their early digital services to widespread indifference within their respective industries. All functionally integrated ecosystems started small and built up membership through the fundamental appeal and usefulness of their digital offerings. They succeed because, as digital services, they are not reliant on mass media to gain popularity. They are products of a new multicontextual digital environment in which utility, coupled with mastery of context, builds value in the long run.

2

The Digital Revolution

Principle Two: Context is king.

At the 2013 Consumer Electronics Show in Las Vegas, General Motors announced a move that was unlike any other in the company's 104-year history. Starting with its 2014 models, the carmaker would incorporate smartphone-like applications into its dashboard infotainment systems. GM, however, would not be the maker of the vast majority of these apps. Instead, the company announced plans to launch its own "App Shop," a catalogue of apps that third-party developers will sell or give away free to GM vehicle owners.[1]

Thanks to the GM App Shop, your car doesn't just communicate with your mobile device—your car *becomes* a mobile device with a direct 4G mobile connection. By loosening its control over the dashboards of its cars, GM would become a mobile app retailer and distributor, just like Apple with its App Store and Google with Google Play. The apps in GM's App Shop begin with the car's infotainment functions, but other apps will integrate with the car's telematics—the electronics that control the car's engine, its diagnostics, and other vital functions.

GM's App Shop field-tests and approves each app for inclusion in the store, a process similar to that of Apple and Android. Driver distraction is a paramount concern, which is why you won't get to download a Netflix app or a web browser for use on your dashboard screen. (But such apps might be acceptable on some models' built-in backseat passenger screens.) In early 2013, GM estimated that 22,000 software developers had already downloaded the App Shop platform's software specifications and were exploring ways to join GM's new open digital platform.[2]

When it comes to the digital dashboard, GM has used the App Shop to fundamentally change the context of its relationship with its vehicles. It has stepped back from its century-old tradition of pushing GM products on its customers and has instead become host, curator, and proprietor of an App Shop filled with other companies' products. This new GM strategy underlines the extent to which the digital revolution represents a *contextual revolution*. In the digital age, context is king.

When Apple introduced a vehicle-compatible voice interface called Siri Eyes Free with its June 2012 iPhone update, the Ford Motor Company denied the new feature access to its SYNC system of in-car mobile connectivity. Why? Because too much of what Siri offers—navigational directions in particular—competes with Ford's own built-in SYNC services. Ford's first priority, typical of the car industry and of most industries, was to protect its own products.[3]

GM's App Shop, in contrast, allows GM vehicles to work with Siri Eyes Free, even though the product is a direct competitor to OnStar, GM's own proprietary voice-command system. Breaking with the manufacturing tradition exemplified by Ford, GM has chosen to make utility its top priority, a perspective more typical of Functional Integration. User acceptance and satisfaction are paramount in a functionally integrated ecosystem, and today's drivers expect to have access to whichever service they find most useful. By opening the App Shop, GM has entered the multicontextual world in which building relationships with customers and partners is more important than moving products. For example, if GM were to protect OnStar by blocking Siri Eyes Free, it would send the wrong signal to those 22,000 prospective developers for the App Shop platform. GM would risk stifling App Shop innovation, which in turn would limit the App Shop's appeal to developers and customers alike.

That's a multicontextual perspective that stands in stark contrast to Ford's product-first orientation. "If we've learned anything from the tech industry," GM vice president Nick Pudar explained, "it's that the people willing to eat their own lunch are the ones who win in the end."[4] From Pudar's point of view, if Siri Eyes Free and other apps prove to be superior to GM's existing OnStar services, OnStar subscription revenues might fall, but it would be a small price to pay if the decision helped confirm the utility of GM's open digital platform.[5]

Ford was a leader in the auto industry when it introduced its cellphone-compatible voice-command SYNC system in 2007. In subsequent years, Ford permitted certain music and radio app developers to add software code that enables their apps to play on the SYNC system through a wireless connection with the driver's mobile phone. Makers of popular smartphone apps such as Pandora and Amazon Cloud Player were among those Ford chose to work with in this way.[6]

Like most efforts to put the digital revolution in the driver's seat, Ford's arrangements with app developers have followed this fairly conventional path for new product development. With Pandora, for instance, Ford initiated a carefully considered strategic partnership, just as Ford would with any other vendor. Then Ford promoted Pandora's compatibility with SYNC as another new feature, another horizontal extension in the Ford product line. Ford denied Siri Eyes Free access to its cars even though Apple and Ford have partnered closely on other projects. Ford wants its customers to rely solely on SYNC's voice controls, not Apple's or anyone else's.

Ford's approach shows how customers lose when companies attempt to impose a traditional product strategy on digital mobile services. Ford relies on the comfortable and conventional singular context of business as it has always been practiced, whereas GM has chosen to build its digital platform on its own multicontextual terms.

If the GM way seems to be riskier and more uncertain than Ford's, that's only because digital products and services themselves are by nature disruptive and unpredictable. In truth, Ford's approach is the riskier of the two. If you attempt to develop, produce, and market digital products and services in the same context as you would other products, you are sailing against headwinds that grow stronger every day.

To fully appreciate the challenge that this contextual revolution poses to today's business world, consider that the mode of making and selling products has not changed substantially since the 1880s, when mass production and national product brands were first made possible by the railroads. Throughout the 20th century, success in every industry depended on the faithful execution of product line extensions through horizontal integration. In 1990, just as it had been in 1890, fortunes were built on the reliable process of creating new products and using advertising to sell them. Beginning with the printed pages of newspapers and magazines, advertising expanded to radio in the 1920s and to television in the 1950s. As an industry, advertising barely existed at all in 1880. By 1910, it had grown to 4 percent of U.S. national income, and for the next 60 years, the industry maintained that same small but significant share of the economy.[7]

Television is by far the single most powerful tool in advertising history. Broadcast television and advertising grew up together as TV's Golden Age in the 1950s and 1960s coincided with the halcyon "Mad Men" years in the ad business. This period saw a quickening in the pace of horizontal integration as multitudes of new brands were successfully developed and introduced to the public through this powerful passive medium. Fortune 500 companies grew enormously by identifying new consumer needs, developing products to serve those needs, and relying on TV advertising to create awareness and drive purchase intent. The wheels of commerce were stoked by commercials.

Each type of media supported by advertising serves a singular purpose that represents a singular context. The context of newspapers and magazines is reading. The context of radio is listening. The context of television is watching. These forms of predigital "analog" media occur within a single larger context that unifies the advertising industry in a particular way. All the advertising we've ever consumed in our lives has occurred within advertising's defining context of *interruption*.

The business of advertising is the business of interrupting. Each advertising message we receive take place in this context. Television advertisers alone spend almost $70 billion a year to intrude on whatever programs we've tuned in to watch.[8] Magazine and newspaper ads attempt to distract our attention away from the articles we intend to read. An interruptive message from the radio sponsor forces us to wait for the traffic and weather report.

Advertising is probably the only industry to grow and prosper by excelling as a source of annoyance. Since the dawn of radio and TV, commercials have been the frequent butt of ridicule and parody because of this mild absurdity. We "pay" for our favorite shows on broadcast media by paying attention to interruptive messages that we would ordinarily ignore *if they were presented in any other context*.

A lot is riding on the context of interruption. When advertising messages lose their power to gain our attention through interruption, products fail, horizontal integration slows, and corporate profits wither. In this sense, the context of interruption has been the linchpin of the consumer economy for more than a century. With stakes that high, advertising agencies over the years became very proficient at the art of interruption. What has been known as "the creative revolution" in advertising during the 1950s and 1960s involved three competing ideas about how interruption can be practiced most effectively.

David Ogilvy, one of the visionary figures of this era, ran an ad agency whose TV spots and print ads were characterized by plain-spoken honesty. Their strategy involved interrupting the consumer with an air of dignity, intelligence, class, and style. Bill Bernbach pioneered the use of high-toned humor in advertising, typified by the clever "Think Small" ads for the Volkswagen Beetle. Leo Burnett conceived the TV commercial as a 30-second story reinforcing the core product idea ("Frosted Flakes — they're great!" and "Only good-tasting tuna get to be Starkist"). The metaphorical stars of such long-running ad campaigns included some of the great icons of advertising history: Tony the Tiger, Charlie Tuna, the Marlboro Man, the Green Giant, the Pillsbury Doughboy, the Energizer Bunny, Aunt Jemima, Betty Crocker, and Ronald McDonald.

With so much talent and so many resources dedicated to the context of interruption, the advertising-driven formula for growth and profits has long worked equally well for nearly all consumer product categories, from cars to cosmetics to cat food. Assisted by their ad agencies and media partners, some of the world's biggest brand names are the unabashed masters of interruption, including Coca-Cola, Procter & Gamble, General Motors, General Electric, AT&T, and American Express.

When, in the 1970s, the spread of cable television began to fragment the media marketplace, a new generation of ad agencies rose to the challenge by making their interruptive messages more exciting and enjoyable. Upstart agencies like Wieden + Kennedy, Goodby Silverstein, and Bartle Bogle Hegarty recognized that the only way to hang on to viewers armed with remote controls and more than a hundred alternative channels was to interrupt entertainment programming with skillfully made pieces of entertaining advertising. Extravagantly expensive and spectacular TV commercials resulted, buoyed by the use of celebrity talent that included Michael Jackson and Madonna for Pepsi, Michael Jordan for Nike, and an entire roster of beautiful spokesmodels for L'Oreal Paris. All media at that time were of the single-context variety.

The first multicontextual media environments in human history entered U.S. homes in the 1980s with the arrival of proprietary online systems such as Compuserve, Prodigy, and America Online. For an America Online "page," as with most web pages or mobile apps, there is no single context. The most popular websites and apps contain within them a multitude of contexts and capabilities. An ordinary local news website, for example, offers text, audio, video, two-way communication through reader comments, and links to countless other sites. Each represents one or more separate contexts.

Year One of the World Wide Web arrived in 1993, when the Mosaic web browser opened the Internet to the general public. From an information standpoint, the implications of this revolution are as profound as Gutenberg's printing press. From the standpoint of advertising and horizontal integration, the impact was just as profound.

The first principle of Functional Integration, utility, attests to Functional Integration's power of attraction. The second principle, multiple contexts, attests to Functional Integration's power of disruption and transformation. One of the most notable qualities of digital media's multiple contexts is a high level of resistance to interruption — that linchpin on which so many billions in product sales depends. Before the opening of the Internet to the public, interruption was once the sole context in which marketing and advertising communications could possibly occur. With the arrival of the digital age, interruption has become just one of many contexts — and one that ranks at the very bottom in terms of consumer appeal. Horizontal integration can't thrive without advertising, advertising can't thrive without interruption, and interruption can't thrive in a multicontextual world in which it is the least attractive context.

○ Ten Contexts for the New Digital Age

The contextual revolution that began with desktop PCs has found its fullest expression on mobile devices. No other consumer technology in history has ever been so quickly and widely adopted as the smartphone — not the automobile, not the radio, not the television, not the computer. There were an estimated one billion smartphones in the world at the end of 2012, and those numbers were expected to double to two billion by 2015.[9] A 2012 survey of American purchasing habits showed that over the previous five years, U.S. consumers had cut back their spending in *every* product category except one: mobile phone bills.[10]

The main reason for the public's rapid embrace of the smartphone is that the smartphone has no single, primary reason for being. Each smartphone means something different to each user. The average U.S. smartphone has forty-one regularly used apps representing a wide range of contexts, with Google Maps, Facebook, YouTube, Twitter, Skype, Yelp, and Instagram ranking high among the most heavily used apps.[11] Categories of usage such as gaming and social networking are among the top activities, along with texting, email, music, shopping, and news. The wide variety of these contexts helps explain why the average smartphone user pauses to look at the device 150 times a day.[12]

All the evolving contexts that drive the lives of digital age consumers can be found on the touchscreen of any smartphone, which suggests that there can be no practical limits to what smartphones will be used for in the future. Because it is hopeless to try to predict the specific capabilities that future smartphone applications will enable, it's all the more important to familiarize yourself with some of the contexts within which those future applications will operate.

From a business standpoint, the value of considering all these contexts is to put yourself in the shoes of a consumer and consider what your company's or brand's role might be in each of these cases. Each of the following ten contexts represents a different way in which a consumer might encounter a brand and call on that brand to deliver back some useful or attractive service, whether it's to gain information, make an e-commerce purchase, locate nearby discounts, suggest a recipe, or help measure athletic performance.

None of these considerations had any relevance to the selling of products and services prior to the emergence of digital technologies such as social networks and mobile devices. Interruption had previously dominated brand conversations because interruption was the only context available for reaching consumers. Now that consumers can interact with brands on a multicontextual basis, interruption is losing its grip, largely because, as we noted, of all the contexts for communication between brands and customers, interruption is the least attractive and by far the least useful.

This is a massive shift that cannot be underestimated. Fortune 500 companies have already spent billions upon billions of dollars to construct and maintain websites, launch mobile apps, and engage in search marketing. (Nearly all of Google's $50 billion in annual revenues are raised from search marketing.) Technologies are creating rising expectations (and opportunities) for brands to play a much broader and more meaningful role in the lives of consumers.

For this precise reason, the contextual revolution has cleared the way for Functional Integration to emerge as a business model that accommodates the consumer's preference for choosing the contexts with which he or she wants to engage. These digital contexts (alone and in mashed-up combinations) contribute to the formation of a new digital terrain on which businesses must learn to engage with their customers. Among the leading brands exercising Functional Integration, these ten contexts rank among the most important:

1. **Information** is the original context of the web, which began as a mechanism for scientists to share their research with each other. This spurred the creation of multitudes of websites that contain information that is published and accessible 24/7 by any user anywhere in the world. Nearly every company's initial foray into digital began with the creation of an informational website about the products and services offered by its brands. Today the information context of the web is exemplified in the form of online search and discovery, which has boosted Google from nowhere to becoming the world's most valuable media brand. Google processes billions of information searches every day, selling targeted advertising in ways that fit more within the context of information than interruption.

2. **Transaction** is the second key context of the digital age, having powered the dot-com revolution of the late 1990s as new businesses emerged (Amazon, eBay) and old ones found even more efficient ways to sell things (Dell, Victoria's Secret). Consumer adoption of e-commerce has transformed the retail world, as more and more purchases are made outside the confines of physical store environments. The context of

transaction also highlights the way in which contexts are amalgamated as mash-ups in the multicontextual digital environment. Amazon, for example, functions primarily in the context of transaction, but its sales are also powered by the contexts of selection and personalization. In fact, most successful digital ventures represent these kinds of amalgamations of contextual power to create new forms of products and services.

3. **Participation** is the context that has turned the public's relationship to media on its head, transforming ordinary individuals from passive media consumers to active content creators. Media sharing sites like Flickr and YouTube exemplify participation, where users create and share photos and videos with other users; as YouTube reached audience numbers that dwarfed all previous forms of mass media, the consumption of media itself was transformed. The participation context of the digital age exploded further with the rise of social media like Facebook and Twitter, where nearly all the content is developed and shared user to user (although companies and brands can similarly function at the content creator level). This new relationship between individuals and media has created new demands on brands to allow similar participation in their content worlds, while also creating new mechanisms for functionally integrated ecosystems to be shared with new consumers.

4. **Conversation** is a context that might be considered a subset of participation. It deserves its own discussion, however, because digital technology enables one-to-many flows of ideas and opinions that can be virally shared with ever greater numbers of participants. A single comment tweeted from an individual with tens of thousands of followers can set off a chain reaction that might tank a movie marketing budget of tens of millions of dollars — or set off a massive protest in

Brazil or a revolution in the Middle East. Thanks to the speed at which social media conversations take place, such real-time dialogues are where increasing numbers of people first hear of breaking news stories.

5. **Application** is the core context of digital services in general and of Functional Integration in particular. As a context, application refers to branded software that is used to provide individualized utility to consumers. Nike+, iTunes, and L'Oreal Paris's My Signature Beauty are all examples of the context of application. The ability of a brand to provide automated, customized services to consumers is a concept entirely new to the digital age. Aspects of other contexts can be delivered *through* the context of application — such as information, transaction, participation, and conversation. The capability of application to deliver other such contexts is a testament to the power of application as a context. When designed and used properly, this context is responsible for an entirely new vision of relationship marketing — one based on producing "owned" and "earned" media for companies.

6. **Location** as a context has been bolstered by the incorporation of GPS technology into smartphones. It points to the growing abilities of brands to interact with consumers at the point of sale — providing advice, user reviews, promotions, price shopping, and even transactions right at the retail point of sale. Google Wallet and other mobile payment platforms that link with retail offers and loyalty programs are growing their capabilities in this context, and services like Foursquare and Yelp rely on it to help their users find recommended destinations within particular geographical areas.

7. **Diversion**, more than any other new media context, has done the most to undermine the advertising context of interruption. Increasingly, consumers go online to snack and nibble on bite-size pieces of entertainment, and many brands have

seized this opportunity to create viral content that is seen by millions, yet requires no paid media to drive its consumption (although others pay to advertise with viral content on YouTube and other video sites). This new behavior of media consumption drives massive audiences on YouTube, Buzz-Feed, Funny or Die, and a host of other sites that deliver these bits and pieces of entertainment, although some brands offer diversion within their own websites and other owned media destinations. The context of diversion relies on other contexts for its effectiveness. Most of us are alerted to viral content through postings on Facebook (context of participation) or tweets on Twitter (context of conversation). This interconnection of multiple contexts in order to spread news and promote new content represents one of the most profound forces of change in the digital age.

8. **Aggregation and distribution** describe the context in which digital technology has supersized all forms of media, not just the diversionary kind. YouTube, Flickr and other media venues distribute billions of pieces of audio and video content all over the world, at no distribution cost to the creators. The disruptive effect this context has had on the field of marketing is hard to overstate. Prior to the emergence of the web and these delivery mechanisms, all marketers were beholden to paid media and the context of interruption as the only means by which to deliver content to potential (or existing) customers.

9. **Visualization** is a useful context, often found within application, as a way to express data so that people can understand and track their fitness, nutrition, and health — including financial health. Services like Mint provide visualizations that tell users how they are spending their money and how their spending compares with others. Visualization within applications helps users understand their energy consumption, their

taste preferences (with FlavorPrint), and even their social participation. Klout and other services, for instance, provide visual representations of your "social standing" according to a participation metric. The ability to track one's personal data is a huge motivator in changing behavior, and, as we've seen with Nike+, helping customers succeed in behavior change can be a tremendous aid to brand loyalty at a time when brand loyalty is generally on the wane.

10. **Gamification** is related to visualization, turning visualized data into "addictive" games often played out through the context of participation. Foursquare is a social network that "gamifies" visits to locations by rewarding the accumulation of visits with various badge awards. Nike+ FuelBand has created a game around Fuel points, and the original Nike+ Running enabled users to create challenges for themselves or others, with trophies and awards for successful completion. All of these awards, whether in Foursquare or Nike+, can be shared via connected social networks like Facebook, Twitter, or Path—further rewarding players with "likes," comments, and "retweets."

And yes, **interruption** remains an important context, but it's one that plays a subordinate role in Functional Integration. Our own experience tells us that interruptive digital display ads, email blasts, and branded SMS texts all enjoy higher response rates when they offer some degree of utility, principle one of Functional Integration. We have seen, for instance, how a digital ad for L'Oreal Paris enjoys a higher click rate when it explicitly offers a click-through portal to My Signature Beauty. Digital consumers respond to the message because they detect its relevant utility. In this sense, the context of interruption can work well if, instead of pushing a message at you, it offers to introduce you to a useful and interesting multicontextual environment. Interruption is not such an intrusion if it informs you about a functionally integrated digital service, a service that is about *you*.

Many of the services that make up Functional Integration are mash-ups of these ten contexts. FlavorPrint is application + visualization + personalization. Nike+ is application + visualization + location (with the GPS-enabled products). When Google first created location-based searches for shops and restaurants, it did so by merging the preexisting contexts of information and location, unlocking billions of dollars in ad revenue. Most of those dollars were diverted from the budgets of traditional, interruptive media advertising.

Mash-ups of these and other contexts ensure that new variations of digital contexts are born nearly every day. All the singular media contexts historically provided by newspapers, magazines, radio, and television are now mashed up on smartphones and in more satisfying on-demand formats — and with considerably less interruption from advertising than before. Smartphone users on average spend more than two hours per day using apps and another hour per day surfing the web. They actively block out marketing messages at every chance they get, while at the same time consuming more media than ever.

These new consumer behaviors produce a drag on the power of horizontal integration to deliver growth and profits, because effective delivery of interruptive advertising relies on certain levels of predictability in consumer media habits. During the 1960s, in particular, the consumer's attention was easy to capture because all analog media offerings were so meager in scope and number. There was the morning newspaper, drive-time radio, and a handful of magazines shared by most middle-class American households. For homemakers, the three commercial television networks offered daytime talk shows, game shows, and soap operas. For families in the evenings, the networks presented primetime dramas, comedies, and variety shows to audiences numbering in the tens of millions. At the height of its popularity in the 1950s, an episode of *I Love Lucy* (and its commercial sponsors) would gain the attention of 11 million U.S. households at a time when the nation only had 15 million sets.[13]

The success of advertising (and, by extension, horizontal integration) has depended on these two all-but-extinct conditions: predictable patterns of media consumption and scarcity of media outlets. Why, after all, are advertising messages found in such rigorously templated formats as the full-page ad, the 15-second radio spot, and the 30-second television commercial? It's because analog media has always derived value from its relative scarcity. There are only so many pages found in a newspaper or magazine, and only so many minutes of commercial time available during an episode of a hit television show or in the course of a radio broadcast day. Advertising templates parcel out discrete portions of these precious pages and broadcast minutes in order to achieve just the right balance of attractive content and commercial interruptions.

So where is the scarcity and predictability in an online world that offers limitless quantities of free information and entertainment? They are nowhere to be found. There are countless news sites and blogs as alternatives to print media. Streaming music sites and podcasts provide convenient alternatives to radio, while Netflix, premium cable, and DVRs continue to chip away at the dwindling broadcast television audience. The fragmentation of the media landscape has led to the strange circumstance in which television advertising prices continue to climb even as television ratings plummet. The absence of large audiences for national brands to reach with their ads has made television's shrinking audiences more valuable than ever.[14]

In the digital media world, where abundance and unpredictability prevail, templated advertising is conspicuously out of place. In fact, there are few templates of any kind to shape our thinking about the multiple contexts of the digital age. In this shift from analog to digital, business has lost the power to set the terms of its relationships with consumers. All the power has naturally shifted from the marketer to the consumer.

Corporate leaders have been slow, for the most part, to awaken to this reality. (Consider the 2012 survey which showed that two-thirds of Fortune 500 CEOs have no personal social media presence.[15]) With interruptive advertising on the wane, and with the century-old formula of "new product + mass media = profits" faltering, many have sought to export their old formula to developing nations, where they hope to find new populations for their vast horizontal product portfolios. In mature markets, companies have pursued that rapid, almost frantic run-up of new products and new brand extensions we noted in the Introduction. They have chosen to increase the volume and pace of new product introductions in the hope that one or two might hit the target amid a blizzard of misses.

With the odds of a hit product grower ever longer, marketers are making more bets and spreading them more widely throughout the marketplace. But introducing new products and new varieties only serves to aggravate the underlying problem of commoditization. Consumers, who are already empowered in so many new ways by the digital revolution, have been given such a wide variety of purchasing options that they retain all the pricing power, leaving almost none for the makers of thoroughly commoditized products.

The digital age is the age of consumer control. Consumers growing up in the digital age are accustomed to manipulating media as they resist being manipulated. The very same digital technologies that created this multicontextual world also provide the means to control the flow of marketing messages, through pop-up blockers, spam filters, DVRs, and other tools. For all these reasons, consumers have expectations of companies and brands that differ markedly from prior expectations in the 20th century. Consumers expect digital technology to offer them authentic value — what we regard as utility in Functional Integration terms. Consumers also expect that whatever utility or value they are offered will reflect the multicontextual reality they experience whenever they pick up their smartphones, 150 times per day.

To deliver growth for brands and profits for their companies, Functional Integration requires the orchestration of multiple digital contexts to create new value for consumers. To take back pricing power in a digital age, functionally integrated brands (such as Nike, in particular) have switched from being masters of interruption to being masters of context. They have changed their relationships with their customers and chosen new approaches in order to gain a grasp of which contexts offer their customers the greatest value, the most utility, the best experience.

o The Eve of Disruption

In February 2012, Bill Ford, the executive chairman of the Ford Motor Company, became the first auto executive ever to give the keynote address at the telecom industry's annual Mobile World Congress in Barcelona. The great-great-grandson of Henry Ford told the crowd that he saw both the automotive and the telecom industries at a crossroads.

"One hundred years ago, the automobile redefined personal mobility," Ford said. "Today, portable communication devices are redefining personal mobility. And I believe that in the future, we will redefine personal mobility together." Ford claimed that "now is the time for us all to be looking at vehicles on the road the same way we look at smartphones, laptops and tablets; as pieces of a much bigger, richer network."[16] By merging transportation and wireless technologies, he said, urban transportation networks could become more efficient and offer more convenient alternatives to the private car.

Henry Ford's legacy was that he did more than anyone to make car ownership an important part of the American Dream. Now, a century later, one of his descendants has become a prominent advocate for putting car ownership into a new, broader social context, as just one piece of a transportation network in a mobile networked world.

For the car industry, the writing is on the wall. The number of miles driven in the United States peaked in 2005 and dropped steadily every year thereafter, largely because young people are losing interest in cars and driving. A 2011 study from the University of Michigan showed that almost one-third of all U.S. nineteen-year-olds had not bothered to get driver's licenses. In 1983, the share of nineteen-year-olds without licenses was just 13 percent.[17]

Throughout the developed world, car culture is fading. Another study by the same Michigan researchers tracked the driving habits of young people in 15 countries and discovered that higher rates of Internet usage tracked very closely with reduced rates of driver's license acquisition. The report's conclusion suggests that "access to virtual contact reduces the need for actual contact among young people."[18]

Early casualties of the digital age included the music and newspaper industries. Could the auto industry be another? In four short years, from 2007 to 2011, the U.S. age demographic most likely to buy a car shifted from the 35-to-44 group to the 55-to-64 group.[19] The shift could indicate a permanent change in car-buying habits among younger adults. Newspaper editors and record executives were slow to grasp how the Internet had changed the contexts of reading news and listening to music. Now carmakers need to understand that smartphones and other mobile devices have shattered the singular context of transportation into a dozen or more digital contexts. For growing numbers of young people today, buying a car makes no more sense than buying a compact disc or a daily newspaper.

One new context of auto-mobility that holds some near-term promise for the car industry is the context of sharing. Mobile and GPS technology makes it easy for urban residents in particular to trade in their cars for inexpensive memberships in car-sharing companies such as Zipcar. Hourly reservations are made online, and access to the cars is gained by an electronic card, with none of the fuss and paperwork of the car rental office. In 2013, more than 760,000 Zipcar members were sharing 10,000 cars on college campuses and cities in the United States, Canada, Great Britain, Spain, and Austria.[20]

Ford earned some points for forward thinking back in 2011 when it entered into a partnership with Zipcar to put 1,000 Ford vehicles in car-sharing sites on college campuses. At the time, however, the move was seen as a promotional and marketing strategy, to expose young students to Ford vehicles, in hope of future sales.[21] (As part of the deal, Ford made an investment in Zipcar, which paid off less than two years later when Avis bought Zipcar for $500 million in cash.[22])

Daimler AG, parent company of Mercedes-Benz, went a step further in 2008 and started its own car-sharing company, called Car2Go, which is stocked with Daimler's tiny two-door Smart cars in 13 North American cities, including Toronto and San Diego, and a dozen other cities in Europe.[23] Speaking at the 2012 Consumer Electronics Show (CES), Daimler chairman Dieter Zetsche joked, "Some colleagues still think that car-sharing borders on communism. But if that's the case, *viva la revolución!*" Projected on the screen behind Zetsche was a gigantic image of Latin American revolutionary Che Guevara.[24]

That sight gag points to a serious reality. Many in the car industry consider car-sharing a downright subversive idea, because promoting the ethos of sharing cars is likely to reduce the appeal of buying cars. "Our car company *sells* cars," conventional thinking goes. "We should not encourage people to share them." Orthodox reasoning and retrogressive objections of this kind are sure to confront every executive attempting to move a company's vision toward the new multicontextual world.

Most people who built their careers in the analog world tend to mistake its singular one-dimensional contexts for simple, objective reality. One fatal flaw in such thinking is that in a multicontextual age, competition can emerge from just about anywhere. Companies that fail to follow their customers into these new contexts are the ones who suffer the most from digital disruption. It is telling that one of the earliest and largest investors in Zipcar was Steve Case, founder of America Online. Case had no experience in the automotive industry, but he knew all about digital disruption. Zipcar's founders understood that many people consider their cars to be expensive but necessary evils. For infrequent drivers, particularly in urban areas, car-sharing offers the chance to escape costly loan and insurance payments while sacrificing little in the way of mobility. A city-backed study of Baltimore Zipcar members showed that nearly one-fifth of them sold their cars after joining.[25]

In his CES speech, Dieter Zetsche invoked cloud computing as a similarly sensible concept. Car-sharing, he said, is like cloud mobility. You don't need to own a computer to access many gigabytes of data, and similarly, you don't need to own a car to have access to one. Some months after Zetsche's speech, Daimler made a $10 million investment in Carpooling.com, the world's largest ride-sharing platform, which connects one million riders with drivers each month in 40 countries.[26] Daimler has also purchased a 15 percent stake in the MyTaxi mobile app,[27] and its Business Innovation lab has sponsored development of a mobility platform called Moovel, which gives users a single digital site for comparing travel options—driving, transit, car-sharing, ride-sharing, taxi, and cycling.[28]

For a century, automakers, car dealers, and advertisers devoted themselves to "moving the metal," with a single-minded focus on selling units through emotionally appealing television advertising. Carmakers still spend $30 billion annually on advertising, and although the trends are toward mobile advertising and away from analog media, the overall approach hasn't changed much.[29] The car-buying environment, however, has changed a lot. Not only are younger people not buying, but the people who are buying no longer nurture the sense of brand loyalty they once did. *Consumer Reports'* 2013 Car-Brand Perception Survey showed that when it comes to leading brands Toyota, Ford, Honda, and Chevrolet, "the perceived difference between brands is shrinking" in terms of safety, quality, value, and other criteria.[30] These digital age buyers have become increasingly practical about cost and fuel efficiency, and these bottom-line concerns have only helped spread commoditization throughout the industry.

Any carmaker hoping to gain market share in the face of these forces needs to engage with the new digital contexts as a primary means of brand differentiation. If cars themselves have become commoditized, as *Consumer Reports* suggests, then car companies should regard their product lines of vehicles as pieces of larger, functionally integrated ecosystems of products and services. GM, through its App Shop and some other initiatives, is clearly moving in this direction.

For example, GM has partnered with Relay Rides, an innovative car-sharing start-up that allows private citizens to rent out their personal vehicles by the hour or by the day. Relay Rides provides a digital marketplace for excess capacity, similar to StubHub's site for selling unwanted sports and theater tickets. Most Relay Ride reservations and transactions take place online. The only real hassle is the pickup and delivery of the car keys. But thanks to

GM's OnStar system and RemoteLink smartphone app, GM cars in the Relay Rides program can be unlocked and started without any need for car keys at all. Renters need only to receive codes sent to their smartphones in order to gain access to the cars they've selected.[31]

GM isn't making any money through this mash-up of sharing and transaction contexts (car owners use Relay Rides as a source of added income). Relay Rides does, however, provide a strong real-world example of RemoteLink's possibilities. GM vice president Nick Pudar says that if a car rental agency wanted to develop the right apps for the GM App Shop, rented GM cars could be personalized for their drivers at a moment's notice. Conceivably, you could save all your personal driving settings to an app on your phone. Then, when you use that app to unlock the rental car's doors, all your navigation destinations, your Internet radio settings, seat heights, and air conditioning preferences would be preloaded and waiting for you. Any apps you had previously purchased and downloaded from GM's App Shop would appear for you in any rented GM car, anywhere in the world.[32]

At that point, owning and driving a GM car would be just one of many contexts in your experience of the GM brand. Just as Apple's App Store is a centerpiece of Apple's ecosystem of value, with the Apple iMac and iPhone tools for running the apps, GM's App Shop might play the same role in the carmaker's future. GM officials have no doubt noted Apple's enormous pricing power over rival makers of PCs, smartphones, and tablets. Apple fans are willing to pay more in order to deepen their experience with Apple's ecosystem. GM, in an industry plagued by commoditization, would do well to follow Apple's example.

BMW's efforts in the direction of Functional Integration are noteworthy for their great variety and for the sheer number of contexts they embrace. At the core of BMW's digital offerings is its ConnectedDrive family of services, which includes dashboard functionality for a limited set of smartphone apps such as Twitter, Yelp, and Pandora; a smartphone app for unlocking your car and finding it in parking garages; real-time traffic information; and a "driver profile" that resets the seats, radio channels, and contact data for each driver in the family.

At the same time, BMW has funded a New York–based venture capital incubator called BMW i Ventures, with the mission to invest in mobility-oriented services that don't necessarily involve car ownership at all. With $100 million in seed money from the parent company, the fund has invested in developing apps for keeping track of children outside the home, delivering real-time public transit information, and finding on-street parking spaces. It's also funding BMW's nascent DriveNow car-sharing system in San Francisco and a handful of German cities. "As megacities become bigger, people have mobility needs, but they satisfy them in different ways," said Bernhard Blaettel. "It doesn't mean we're convinced cars are going to become less important. We just think that in some areas they may be used in a different context." BMW strategist Joerg Reimann offered, "We want to become future-proof."[33]

BMW's boldest attempt at Functional Integration involves transforming the BMW key fob into an electronic transit pass, a hotel key card, and a potential substitute for a credit card. Using NFC (near-field communications) technology, the key fob would electronically store the codes needed to conduct all kinds of transactions, including purchases at stores offering "contactless" credit card payments. BMW officials speculate that your car key fob might someday replace your house key and your company ID card.[34]

One near-term role for the NFC-enabled key fob is as a substitute for easily lost hotel room key cards. In a partnership with VingCard Elsafe, a leading company in hotel entry systems, BMW has tested a service that allows drivers to find a hotel through the

ConnectedDrive navigation service and book a room online while driving. A code sent to the key fob would allow you to access your room directly, without ever checking in at the front desk.[35] The vision is one in which a series of frictionless transactions take you seamlessly from the driver's seat into your hotel room, all within the care of BMW's ecosystem—and with the smallest role being played by the car itself.

3

The Ecosystem of Value

Principle Three: Synergy captures customers.

In 1999, Apple Computer had fallen on such hard times that its share of the global personal computer market had dwindled to below 3 percent.[1] Top executives at rival companies had publicly declared Apple all but dead. Software developers had grown reluctant to write versions of their applications for Apple's Macintosh operating system because Apple offered them so few potential customers. Ironically, it was rejection by one such software maker that put Apple on the path to becoming the world's most valuable company.

At the time, the digital graphics company Adobe sold a popular video-editing software program called Adobe Premiere. When Apple founder and CEO Steve Jobs asked Adobe to develop an Apple-compatible version of Premiere for the forthcoming Macintosh OSX operating system, Adobe officials turned him down.

There just weren't enough Macintosh users to make the effort worthwhile, they explained. The rejection left Jobs feeling stunned and angered because Adobe and Apple had a long history of working together. In fact, Premiere had first been introduced in 1991 as a Macintosh-only application.

But the slight by Adobe was also a sobering experience for Jobs. Forced to make a virtue of necessity, Jobs had the insight that would change Apple's destiny forever. He decided that certain pieces of software and hardware critical to Apple's future should no longer be dependent on third parties. By making it a general principle for Apple to create seamless, end-to-end user experiences, from software to hardware, Jobs saw that he would not only make his customers happier but also avoid being at the mercy of software makers like Adobe.[2]

A year later, when Apple released OSX, the new operating system was delivered with a suite of free software applications that included iTunes, iMovie 2, and iDVD. The Macintosh, Jobs announced at the 2001 Macworld conference, had a new role in the home. The desktop computer, he said, would become a "digital hub for our emerging digital lifestyle."[3] With its big screen, large memory, and high processing speeds, the personal computer would serve as a central home base for new digital gadgets such as the portable mp3 player, the digital movie camera, and the portable DVD player.

All the applications in Apple's digital hub were designed to work easily with each other. You could make a playlist on iTunes, import it as the soundtrack with iMovie, and then burn a copy of your finished home movie with iDVD. (Apple would add iPhoto a year later.) Although the new digital hub contained certain functionally integrated elements, Apple was still operating out of the old horizontal integration playbook. The applications in the digital hub were marketed as part of a new Apple product line. Their chief role was to increase the appeal of buying a new Mac.

It took several more years before the digital hub evolved to become a driver of Apple profits on its own. Apple added the iPod as a complement to iTunes in 2001 and then opened the iTunes digital music store in 2003. By 2006, Apple was earning more revenue from iPod sales than from desktop computers. Apple's revenues, which had fallen to a 12-year low of $5.36 billion in 2001, grew sixfold to $32.48 billion in 2008 with the introduction of the iPhone.[4] By then, Apple had erased the word "computer" from its corporate name. Within seven short years, Apple's digital hub had transformed the entire company and developed into what we would call a functionally integrated *ecosystem of value*.

○ Greater Than the Sum of Its Parts

In strategic terms, Apple's initial attempt to leverage sales of desktop computers through the digital hub was a variation on the age-old "razor-razorblades" business model pioneered by Gillette at the turn of the 20th century. Gillette became the leading maker of shaving products by giving away razors and then selling high-margin, patented razor blades that fit only those razors. Apple's digital hub started out as a sort of "reverse-razorblade" model. Apple offered iTunes and the other free applications with OSX in order to stimulate new sales of high-margin desktop computers. And because iMovie 2 and iDVD worked best with additional processing power, they also motivated certain loyal Apple Macintosh fans to get rid of their old Macs and invest in new hardware.

The digital hub represented only one of many attempts by Steve Jobs to reassert Apple's relevance in the personal computer industry. Jobs had returned to Apple as CEO in 1997, having been fired 12 years earlier. He took over a company teetering on the brink of total failure. Less than 4 percent of all desktop computers shipped worldwide in 1997 were running Apple software, with

Microsoft-compatible computers occupying almost all of the remaining market.[5] Microsoft could have eliminated Apple as a competitor by simply ceasing production of Apple-compatible versions of Microsoft's popular Word, Excel, and PowerPoint office applications. But Microsoft avoided taking that drastic step and became an Apple investor instead. That's because if Apple were to go under, Microsoft would become a monopoly, subject to breakup under federal antitrust laws. Apple owed its entire existence to Microsoft's need to perpetuate the illusion of competition.[6]

The new iTunes digital music library turned out to be the biggest hit among the various digital hub applications. Although iTunes earned rave reviews for its ease of use, that ease of use suffered when it came to transferring music files to portable mp3 players, which were emerging in growing numbers. Jobs and his team decided to make an Apple-branded digital player of their own, designed to sync easily with iTunes, as a way of extending their goal of seamless user experiences. The iPod, which was brought to market in October 2001, owed its name to the small one-man pod vehicles that docked with the mother ship in *2001: A Space Odyssey*.[7]

The iPod was an instant hit, but it had one serious limitation that was outside Apple's control. The only way to load new songs via iTunes was either to copy the songs from CDs or, as was becoming increasingly common, to obtain pirated copies online. Apple began conversations with recording company executives about the idea of selling digital music through iTunes, but the executives were wary. Jobs's idea of selling songs digitally at 99 cents was potentially disruptive to recording industry profits, which relied on CD sales of whole albums. If consumers bought only the songs they liked, there was a danger that revenues would tumble. Rampant pirating had made recording executives hostile to digitized music in general and to Apple in particular. A bold 2001 ad for iTunes headlined "Rip. Mix. Burn." had been denounced by some music executives as a blatant invitation to music piracy.[8]

Apple's greatest weakness, however, turned out to be a strength in this case. The recording companies determined that Apple's tiny market share of the computer industry made it a safe place to experiment with such a dangerous idea.[9] On April 28, 2003, the iTunes Music Store opened with a library of 200,000 tracks and with all five of the top music labels participating.

The iTunes Music Store was the puzzle piece that turned Apple's digital hub into a true ecosystem of value. Just like an ecosystem in nature, each piece in the ecosystem of value affects all the others. When a consumer adds a new piece of Apple software or hardware, the new piece adds value to all the other pieces within that ecosystem. Taken together, all the pieces of an ecosystem of value are worth more than the sum of their parts—the very definition of synergy.

The quality of synergy is what distinguishes a functionally integrated ecosystem of value from a horizontally integrated product line. Horizontal integration achieves success by maximizing profits through the sale of products in target-marketed consumer niches. Functional Integration, by contrast, depends on building relationships with loyal groups of consumers who become participants and evangelists for the entire interconnected ecosystem of products and services.

Functional Integration succeeds only by delivering consistent customer value. It challenges you to increase the value of your entire ecosystem by thinking in terms of synergy with each additional new service, new product, software revision, or product update. The goal is to grow the total amount of value that accrues to your best customers, so that deeper usage by the customer leads to the enjoyment of greater value within the ecosystem.

Contrast Apple's approach with that of a typical horizontally integrated firm like Sony. Inside Sony, marketing teams representing a vast portfolio of products chase after a diverse range of customers with little concern for the interoperability of those products and little interest in the total value equation presented to the customer. Successful Functional Integration strategies are mindful of product categories, price points, and other marketing concerns, but racking up sales within individual product lines is not the primary objective. In an ecosystem, better performance in one area should be designed to create new value and profits in other areas. Improvements to iTunes software might prompt better iPod sales. Selling more iPods drives more revenue to the iTunes Music Store. Synergy, so often cited as the elusive payoff for breaking down corporate silos, is actually a normal by-product of ecosystems—in nature and in Functional Integration.

In the case of these business ecosystems of value, synergy is impossible without the glue of membership in digital services such as iTunes, Amazon Prime, and Nike+. Availability of membership in digital services is ultimately what sets these companies apart from product-oriented competitors such as Sony, Walmart, and Adidas. The digital music store made iTunes into more than a music library, and it made the iPod more than just another digital music player. All three made the Mac into something more than the typical commodity-like Windows PC.

From a brand perspective, Apple's development of its ecosystem also demonstrates how these interconnected products and services create multiple entry points *into* the brand. For many consumers, the iPod was their first doorway into the Apple ecosystem. Once a version of iTunes was developed to work on Microsoft Windows, multitudes of consumers who had never owned a Macintosh entered Apple's ecosystem with the relatively low-cost iPod purchase. Even as the Macintosh continued to languish in terms of computer market share, the iPod grabbed an early overwhelming market share among digital music players. Apple Inc. made profits through its ecosystem in ways that Apple Computer never could. And because the iTunes Music Store provided Apple with an additional revenue stream, Apple was able to reduce prices on low-end versions of the iPod because getting more people to join the ecosystem made it all the more valuable to Apple's bottom line. In the final quarter of 2006, total iPod-related revenues, including those from the iTunes Music Store, were almost twice as high as Apple's revenues from Mac computer sales. In January 2007, Apple removed the word "computer" from its official company name.[10]

It was around this time that the lawless "Wild West" aspects of the new digital world began to uncover the inadequacies of Windows computers. As popular admiration grew for Apple's carefully cultivated ecosystem, Windows PC users were growing increasingly impatient with the onslaught of viruses, Trojan horses, spyware, and worms affecting their inexpensive, commoditized machines. The personal computer industry became so competitive on price that user experience suffered, one of the inevitable outcomes of commoditization driven by horizontal integration.

When Sony, for instance, attempted to compete with Apple by launching the Sony Connect online music store in May 2004, the store struggled with buggy software[11] and other problems for three years before shutting down.[12] One problem was internecine fights among Sony's silos. Sony's entertainment division, which owned Columbia Records (and was much more profitable than the digital music division) insisted on such cumbersome copyright restrictions that the few shoppers who entered Sony's digital music store had poor user experiences. Sony's weak attempt to develop an ecosystem to compete with iTunes never gained any traction with music buyers.[13]

Sony's numerous lines of products at all different price points are horizontally integrated to such an extreme degree that the company has never managed to make that vast portfolio achieve the synergies of an ecosystem of value. The total number of Apple products, by contrast, can be displayed on a single conference room table, and each piece contributes to making the other pieces function better.

Why, for instance, did the first Apple iPod work so well? How did such a compact, simple object manage to be so user-friendly? Normally, credit for these qualities in the iPod has gone to Jobs and his team for their love of design, for their genius in keeping the user experience in mind. But this simple assessment, that Apple's team is and was uniquely talented, utterly misses the point. It's much more accurate to say that the iPod was simple to use only because it was one part of Apple's larger ecosystem of value.

At the time of the first iPod's release, most stand-alone mp3 players were comparatively clunky and heavy because of all the electronics they required to carry out their many functions. The iPod was deliberately not conceived as a stand-alone device, so it had certain limitations. When you held an early iPod in your hand, for example, there was no way to sort lists, delete songs, or otherwise organize your music. You needed to sort and organize lists on your desktop iTunes application, then sync the iPod with the desktop. Competing portable players could sort lists and do much more, which is why they were so clunky and required saintlike patience to scroll through countless tiny screens and remember which buttons to press.

This was something other electronics makers couldn't understand; or, if they understood it, they still had trouble competing with the iPod. The iTunes application took on the cumbersome functions of sorting and organizing songs, allowing the iPod to remain a simple and "insanely great" product. The first-generation iPod's sported a hefty $399 price tag when it was introduced in 2001, which led many to doubt its prospects for success. Competing digital music players were much cheaper, and some could perform more functions, such as playing mini-CDs. But none of the rival players sold as well as the iPod, especially after the opening of the iTunes store. By September 2009, Apple had a 73.8 percent market share of digital music player sales. It had sold 225 million iPods by then, making the iPod one of most popular electronic devices in history.[14] While other digital music players competed on price and features, driving each other's sales and profits downward, iPods could sell at a premium price because they were much more than gadgets. Millions were willing to pay a little more for the iPod because it was the only digital player that offered an entry point to the world's best digital ecosystem.

Years later, Amazon's Kindle would succeed on the same basis. Kindle was the first functionally integrated digital reader. At the time of its introduction, it was the only e-reader that enabled instant downloads from Amazon's digital bookstore over Amazon's wireless service. (Other readers required clumsy and unreliable synchronization with a PC.) The Kindle is an organic extension of Amazon's ecosystem, and when you buy a Kindle, you are buying more than a gadget. You are buying special access to the world's premier e-book library and the entire Amazon ecosystem.

What Apple and Amazon have both achieved with their ecosystems is what Warren Buffett would call "economic moats." Buffett popularized the theory that certain dominant brands are like castles protected by unbreachable moats that give them pricing power and leave competitors at perpetual disadvantage.[15] Coca-Cola's superior brand reputation is one such moat. Vast membership is eBay's moat. Any competitor attempting to storm eBay's castle will find that stealing market share will be difficult because eBay's market position is protected by a moat made up of tens of millions of loyal and satisfied members.

With Functional Integration, the economic moat analogy takes on a somewhat different metaphorical shape. Apple's best customers actually cross the moat, enter the castle, and take center stage in Apple's ecosystem. With functionally integrated companies like Apple, Google, or Amazon, consumers are so well served inside their castles that most never leave. This is true of every functionally integrated digital service that requires registration and membership. Once these members are inside the castle walls, it is very difficult for any competitor to lure them out.

One of the Apple ecosystem's most undervalued assets is the difficulty its users experience in trying to leave it or buy products that are outside it. Android tablets and Kindle Fires are cheaper than comparable iPads and have certain features that iPads lack.[16] However, for someone who already owns an iPhone, the ease of interoperability with the Apple ecosystem almost guarantees that that particular iPhone owner will buy an iPad instead. That's the synergy of the Apple ecosystem in action.

Nonetheless, there are an estimated 20 million Kindle owners, representing 40 percent of Amazon's U.S. customer base. A 2013 survey showed that Kindle owners spend on average $1,233 per year at Amazon, while other Amazon customers average $790 per year. Kindle owners also shop more widely at Amazon. More than half reported buying from seven or more different departments, compared with just 35 percent of non-Kindle owners. These numbers help explain why Amazon prices Kindles so low. Said Mike Levin of Consumer Intelligence Research Partners, "Another way to look at Kindle Fire and Kindle e-Reader is as a portal to Amazon.com."[17]

As value accrues to a consumer within the Apple or Amazon ecosystem, that value becomes all but inelastic—impossible to replace by a competitor. Inelasticity is an important goal in growing the value of the ecosystem. Amazon's popular $79 per year Amazon Prime membership started out as simple annual fee for getting free two-day shipping. Then Amazon opened its video rental service and added free video rentals as an additional benefit of Amazon Prime membership. Next came free borrowing of e-books from the Kindle lending library. Then Amazon went into production of original programming for its video service, accessible only to members of Amazon Prime.

With an estimated global membership of 20 million,[18] Amazon Prime developed into a full-fledged competitor to Netflix, which had 44 million members in early 2014.[19] But unlike the Netflix website, the Amazon ecosystem has multiple points of entry. For some people Amazon Prime is a lending library, for others it's a video service, and for others it's a shipping service. The accreted value of the $79 membership keeps growing every time Amazon expands the ecosystem's range of services. Netflix, the disruptor of the video rental business, now faces disruption at the hands of Amazon, because quitting Amazon Prime, with all its benefits, is much more difficult than quitting Netflix.

The retailing industry, of which Amazon is among the biggest players, suffers more from elasticity than almost any other industry. Retailing has become particularly elastic in the U.S. economy. Store brands and product brands have proliferated to an extent that all kinds of categories have become commoditized at most price points. But thanks to its ecosystem of value, Amazon is perhaps the sole noncommoditized retailer remaining outside the luxury market. There is no real replacement in the mass market for Amazon.

From this perspective, Apple Computer's transformation to Apple Inc. takes on some added significance. Neither Amazon nor Google have limited themselves with product names, either. When Apple formally removed the word "Computer" from the company name in 2007, it marked the beginning of Functional Integration as a new business model. Functionally integrated companies have no reason to identify themselves with any particular product. That's a relic of the horizontal integration age.

○ The Birth of a Tech Company

The recent history of Nike mirrors that of Apple in some important ways. Nike never fell as hard or as fast as Apple did in the late 1990s, but during that same time period, Nike's status as the world's largest maker of athletic footwear came under attack from an increasingly competitive field. In 1980, the year Nike went public, its U.S. market share had reached 50 percent. But by the 1990s, the running shoe industry was beginning to fragment into the wide variety of niche product categories we see today, including fashion running, trail running, lightweight, and minimalist, among others.

Nike responded to these challenges as nearly all companies do, by becoming more horizontally and vertically integrated. It expanded its running shoe portfolio with the creation of Air technology and the Air Max line of products. In 1985, Nike developed a signature basketball shoe bearing the name of NBA rookie phenom Michael Jordan. By the end of the 1980s, Nike had introduced its iconic "Just Do It" brand tagline and expanded into training, golf, and soccer products. Vertical integration at Nike took a big step in 1990, with the opening of the first Niketown store in Portland, Oregon.

Nike's early online marketing efforts were representative of most such projects at the time. The ecosystem model had not yet evolved, and Nike's online presence reflected the company's horizontal orientation. The e-commerce site, called Niketown.com, provided a front door to a series of sites organized by category: NikeRunning.com, NikeBasketball.com, NikeFootball.com, and NikeGoddess.com for women (Nike being the Greek goddess of victory). The Nike site treated the athletes the way Coca-Cola might treat Coke, Diet Coke, and Sprite drinkers, as individuals with distinctive tastes, as separate consumer segments.

Visitors to the subsites of the Nike universe were treated to content derived from the various mass media advertising campaigns running at the time. In retrospect, it's easy to see how this attempt to integrate online media with mass market segmentation and mass media advertising was a flawed strategy. The mass media context of interruption was not particularly welcomed by visitors to a company's own website, and a television advertisement — even a truly great one — was rarely a good starting point for a digital idea. But this was the type of strategy nearly every major brand pursued in the early years of the web.

Even then, consumer sentiment was already beginning to shift away from novelty to utility when it came to digital technology. The appeal of viral videos wore off fast, while the most heavily trafficked websites were conspicuously those that were most *useful*, such as Google search. Increasingly, consumers grew to expect their investment of time and attention with digital media to yield a tangible benefit to their lives in terms of convenience and value. Consumers were ready for brands to engage them the way the rest of the web was engaging them, through information, visualization, and any number of the other contexts of the digital age.

Nike took its first steps in this direction in 2003 and 2004 when NikeRunning.com introduced a set of online database tools for runners. A simple running tracker enabled runners to manually enter and save data about their runs. A second tool enabled marathon runners in training to calculate their split times for each mile, vital in training for a specific goal time. Split times could be printed out so that runners could take them along and check them during their races.

Like the Apple digital hub, here was the kernel of an ecosystem of value. Both tools were rooted in utility that was relevant to Nike customers, and were conspicuously independent of any specific advertising campaign. The drawback, of course, was that these Nike running tools didn't take advantage of the digital contexts available at the time. Each runner using Nike's online tools still needed a stopwatch and a map to measure time and distance, write them down, and then painstakingly enter them manually on the website form. Nike's online tools were only nominally better than simple paper forms.

Nike had been investigating automated measurements of performance for years. In 1987, it had actually introduced a short-lived, cumbersome sonar-based product called Nike Monitor, which measured distance and speed with instruments strapped to a runner's chest. In more recent years, company engineers had toyed with the idea of a "smart shoe" that could detect distance and speed, but they were stymied by the problem of how to save and download the data.

In 2005, Nike engineers noticed the popularity of iPods among runners and determined that the iPod could be the missing link in their smart shoe idea. Partnering with Apple, Nike produced the Nike+ iPod kit. The partnership with Apple made perfect sense: more and more people were listening to music while they ran, and Apple had a commanding market share in portable digital music players. But the iPod also had just enough of an open architecture to allow it to accept a hardware receiver that could take data from the accelerometer in the shoe and store it on the iPod.

A team at R/GA worked side by side with teams at Nike and Apple to develop the Nike+ user experience as well as the Nike+ website. Via the password-protected Nike+ site, users would be able to track their progress over time. They could set goals for themselves (run more, run longer, run faster), but they could also challenge other users of the system. In essence, a community of runners could form around their running data, spurring each other on, participating in events, and competing in challenges.

When the Nike+ iPod kit containing the sensor and iPod receiver was introduced to Nike and Apple retail stores, there was no other competition at its $29 price point. There were GPS-enabled run-trackers available from auto navigation companies like Garmin, but those products cost hundreds of dollars. And they didn't have the marketing muscle of Nike and Apple behind them, not to mention the fan base of Apple's ecosystem. Nike's own ecosystem was incubated from its start through the company's partnership with Apple.

Within its first year on the market, Nike+ was already proving to be a massive success. It lifted the market share of Nike's running shoes almost immediately. Nike sold 1.3 million Nike+ iPod kits in its first two years on the market, and during that time, Nike's market share in running shoes grew from 48 to 61 percent — a remarkable number and one hard to imagine delivering with either a nifty new ad campaign or even a new model of shoe.[20]

As more runners joined Nike+, Nike learned more about the members of its new ecosystem than it had ever known about its ordinary customers. The average length of a run was 35 minutes, for instance, and back in 2009, the most popularly programmed song was "Pump It" by the Black Eyed Peas.[21] The average Nike+ user visited the website three times per week to upload new running data, take a look at progress metrics, exchange friendly "trash talk" with competitors, download new music mixes, and glance at new Nike gear.

In effect, Nike had created an "owned" media channel for runners. "When you have millions of people that come back and reconnect with your brand multiple times a week, you realize that that connection is more valuable and powerful than any traditional pushed marketing messages," said Nike vice president Stefan Olander. "[With Nike+] we created a link stronger than anything we could ever say in our communications."[22] Advertisers typically use reach and frequency as core metrics of an advertising campaign's effectiveness, with reach as the number of people who potentially see the ad and frequency as the number of times they view it. Nike's new media channel had a reach in the millions along with a three-times-per-week frequency, and it operated at a fraction of the cost of advertising.

For the first time in Nike's history, a digital service connected to a legacy category was driving market share growth—at a time when the category was becoming more and more competitive. Nike and R/GA continued to enhance the user experience of Nike+, adding new features and functionality in an ongoing software development process that took note of what services Nike+ users valued most commonly. Nike's new ecosystem had made it as much a tech company as a footwear company, bringing permanent change to the company's entire business strategy.

o Managing the Ecosystem

In growing its ecosystem of value, Nike is doing what the late environmental scientist Donella Meadows regarded as listening to the system and responding to its feedback loops. Meadows's book *Thinking in Systems* tells how managers of all kinds of systems can learn from the ways that ecosystems operate in nature. One central tenet of Meadows's work was that "the *least obvious* part of any [human] system is its function or purpose."[23] Every system contains so many subunits, each working away at its own functions, that the sum effect is often hard to see clearly, much less steer or guide. And yet, Meadows pointed out, the function of a system is the most crucial determinant of any system's behavior.

Nike, for instance, makes and sells footwear, clothing, and sports equipment for athletes. That's the most obvious part of Nike's function and purpose. But Nike's less obvious mission statement is "To bring inspiration and innovation to every athlete in the world." Without proper regard for that stated function and purpose, it is unlikely that there would be a Nike ecosystem (Figure 3.1). If Nike's function and purpose were limited to

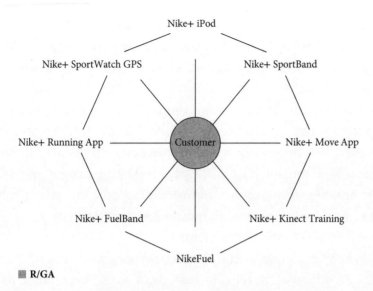

Figure 3.1 Nike's Ecosystem of Value, with the Customer at Its Center

the obvious—the making and selling of stuff—then what the company's systems produced would never rise above that of commodity-grade sporting goods.

Function and purpose are critical for every company or brand hoping to incorporate Functional Integration as a business model. Ecosystems are unpredictable in the way they produce synergies because unpredictability is inherent in the nature of ecosystems. With so many moving parts affecting each other inside the ecosystem, uncertainty is the only constant. Ecosystems are led by listening to and learning from them.

For functionally integrated companies, the advantage of having ecosystem customers residing inside their moated castles is that those customers provide the fast digital feedback loops that enable the right kind of growth for the ecosystem. Ecosystems rely on feedback and are, by their design, ideally suited to provide it. At L'Oreal Paris, for instance, marketers and product researchers learn about their customers' needs from My Signature Beauty just as surely as visitors to the site learn about themselves. Unlike other forms of consumer research, the flow of information about beauty needs within My Signature Beauty is easy to sustain and costs very little.

It is easy to state, as many companies have, that you intend to become "the Amazon of X" or "the iTunes of Y." The results, however, will be at odds with your hopes if the people in your organization remain fixed on targeted consumer categories, rather than building relationships and providing ever-increasing value to the best customers within your ecosystem (thereby attracting more people into your ecosystem).

When Sony's digital music players were competing with Apple in the early days of the iPod, it seemed as though Sony should have had the upper hand in almost every way. The Walkman, after all, was a Sony invention. Why wouldn't the domain of portable digital music players be Sony's to rule? What's more, Sony controlled a major recording label and had marketing resources far superior to that of Apple. But Sony never built a sustainable ecosystem of value. It could not overcome its product-oriented tendencies. Its horizontally integrated bias was baked into the company's culture of separate divisions and product lines. The Sony brand remains highly regarded for its product quality, but it has never found a way to provide enough value to get people to cross the moat, come into its castle, and become a part of a Sony ecosystem. Despite the Sony reputation for excellence, it remains a maker of increasingly commoditized electronics products, losing billions of dollars a year as a result.

This is not to suggest that leaders in Functional Integration such as Apple and Nike have not struggled with questions of purpose and function. The original purpose of the iPod, after all, was to sell more Apple desktop computers. Steve Jobs hung on to this idea long after some of his lieutenants wanted to open iTunes and the iPod to Windows computers. Although Windows commanded more than 95 percent of the computer market, Jobs insisted that the iPod remain an exclusively Apple-based product, in hopes of inducing more people to buy Apple computers. Jobs angrily challenged a team of Apple executives to prove to him that it made business sense to expand the Apple ecosystem to the wider computer universe, before he finally gave in. It wasn't long before revenues from desktop computer sales became just a small part of Apple's overall business.

When the iPhone debuted in 2007, only a handful of Apple-made apps were available on its touchscreen. Jobs was reluctant to open up the phone to apps from third-party developers, even though competitor Nokia had already been doing so on its smartphones for more than a year. Not until July 2008, with the introduction of iOS 2.0, did Apple officially launch the App Store as yet another important piece in its ecosystem. Third-party developers flocked to the platform, earning Apple yet another multibillion-dollar stream of revenue. Within five years, the Apple App Store ballooned to offer 900,000 apps.[24] Apple customers spent more than $10 billion at the App Store in 2013, and by the end of that year, third-party developers had earned more than $15 billion from Apple over the life of the store.[25]

These examples from Apple illustrate how difficult it can be for even the most farsighted of companies to break from the horizontal integration mind-set in the development of an ecosystem of value. Opening the iPod to Windows users and opening the App Store to outside developers are, in retrospect, fairly obvious ways to grow the ecosystem with more users and more entry points. Each move exemplifies the first three principles of Functional Integration: utility, multiple contexts, and synergy. But from the traditional business perspective, expanding the iPod and iTunes to Windows would drag down Apple computer sales. Allowing third-party developers into the iPhone would take away Apple's captive market and relinquish too much power over the user experience. In both cases, Steve Jobs, noted for his visionary nature, was nonetheless prepared to withhold value from the Apple ecosystem in the name of short-term, product-oriented concerns such as sales and control.

Nike faced a similar choice in 2010 when the iPhone provided the company with a way to open Nike+ to all runners, regardless of the brand of shoes they wore. With its built-in GPS and motion-sensing accelerometer, an iPhone had the capabilities of replacing the in-shoe sensor that came with the Nike+ kit. As the iPhone became the eventual market share leader among smartphones, Nike and R/GA began collaborating on a Nike+ running app for the iPhone. The app would enable more accurate tracking of running distance and speed, as well as offer the ability to map a run. With the app's release, anyone could become a Nike+ runner. No Nike+ shoe insert was needed.

This conscious decision to cannibalize sales of the Nike+ iPod kit was partly a competitive decision, one that ensured that no other firm would be tempted to develop a similar app and draw users away from the Nike+ ecosystem. It was also an opportunistic move. It gave Nike the chance to begin developing relationships with consumers who are now outside the Nike ecosystem, to bring them in and introduce them to the entire breadth of Nike's product line. Nike already knew that product sales were boosted by Nike+ members checking in on their running results three times or more per week. There was no point in maintaining a higher price barrier to Nike+ membership with results like those. The Nike+ iPhone app debuted at a cost of $1.99, but later was offered by the App Store at no charge.

Two other examples from Nike show how constant change in technology and digital contexts will determine the usefulness of ecosystem features. Back in 1999, Nike launched a revolutionary new digital service called "i.D.," which stands for "Individually Designed." The www.NIKEiD.com website enabled users to custom-design their own Nike shoes, making a variety of color selections—from base color to shoelace to the color of the Nike swoosh on the side of the shoe. On completion of the customization process and placing of an order, the shoes themselves were manufactured in a custom factory in China and shipped to consumers in six weeks or less. The service captured tons of press attention, but its performance left much to be desired. The web technologies available in 1999 made the shopping process unbearably slow.

It was four years until Adobe's Flash application gave web developers a way to create faster, more immersive technologies online. R/GA went to work with Nike in redeveloping NIKEiD with Flash. The new interface gave users a near-instantaneous ability to view color selections, vastly speeding up the design process. With a simplified interface and improved user experience, a digital service that had languished for years as a failed experiment became a thriving, high-margin, revenue-driving e-commerce channel.

The rise of new digital contexts can similarly offer opportunities to create utility and synergies in an ecosystem. The rise of Facebook and Twitter made for potentially compelling additions to the Nike ecosystem. Facebook, in particular, represented the rapid rise of digital services that users consumed daily, moving more and more aspects of their lives to the digital domain. Upgrades in the Nike+ app and website enabled users to share their running data through Facebook and Twitter. As an added feature, any Facebook member who was also a Nike+ user could easily notify Facebook friends that he or she was about to go for a run. During the run, if any Facebook friend offered a comment or a thumbs-up "like," the runner would be instantly alerted by the motivating sound of cheers and applause. By interoperating with these social networks, Nike+ extends opportunities for Nike runners all over the world to communicate and compete with each other, maintaining its status as a social network in its own right.

In what would be his final keynote address at an Apple developer's conference, Steve Jobs proclaimed in March 2011 that the center of Apple's digital hub had at long last left the desktop. A new service in the Apple ecosystem, iCloud, would take on the role. Less than ten years after the desire to sell more iMacs provided the logic for creating an ecosystem in the first place, the iMac would now become just another device inside the Apple ecosystem, along with the iPad, iPhone, and Apple TV.[26]

One of Jobs's many legacies is the example he set for managing Apple's ecosystem. The chief lesson might be that the never-ending challenge of Functional Integration is always to be looking to create new value and new synergies through utility and the mastery of digital contexts.

o Business Transformation

In the 1850s, the instant communications offered by the telegraph transformed the way business was transacted, and they thoroughly disrupted centuries of business communications traditions. Railroads in the 1880s provided unprecedented access to national markets, transforming the nature of manufacturing, wholesaling, and retailing forever. Now the Internet and Functional Integration pose another equally profound set of changes and choices before today's companies.

It is easy in the short term to disregard threats to the status quo and stick to one's core competencies, even as the products of those competencies are being replaced or commoditized. Theodore Leavitt's famous 1960 *Harvard Business Review* paper, "Marketing Myopia," observed how the railroads doomed themselves to bankruptcy and irrelevance because they continued to believe that they were in the railroad business and not in the broader transportation business. To avoid the railroads' fate, Leavitt counseled, "Management must think of itself not as producing products but as providing customer-creating value satisfactions ... otherwise the company will be merely a series of pigeonholed parts, with no consolidating sense of purpose or direction."[27] The Internet was all but inconceivable when Leavitt wrote this back in 1960, yet his words make as strong a case for Functional Integration as any that you will see.

As Functional Integration gains traction in more companies, it becomes increasingly difficult to classify exactly what business those companies are in. Just about anyone could have told you that Apple was in the computer business in 2002. But what is Apple now? Although it is certainly a tech company, it is also the world's largest retailer of music and a major retailer of digital books, magazines, and movies.

Google and Amazon are technology companies, too, but Google's chief source of revenue is advertising, and Amazon's revenue comes almost entirely from retailing. (Meanwhile, Google is experimenting with self-driving cars, robots, and Google Glass, a form of wearable mobile computing, while Amazon in 2013 began delivering groceries in three West Coast cities.[28]) In Chapter One, we showed how McCormick has begun to explore the digital frontier of flavor and recipes. In Chapter Two, we saw how carmakers are lining up to redefine themselves as tech companies in the transportation business. Could it be that someday not too far in the future, McCormick's FlavorPrint does for recipes what iTunes has done for music? And what business would McCormick be in then?

With such great questions of business transformation facing all these companies, Functional Integration is hardly a job to be left solely to marketing departments, even if that's where most ecosystems of value get their start. Nike+, for instance, began as a marketing idea that rapidly outgrew its original purpose. "Nike+ was an experiment," Nike's Stefan Olander acknowledges, "but good marketing is solving things for people, making things easier and helping people get better at what they want to do. If that works, you can turn it into a service, when it becomes a service it becomes a component of your business."[29] Olander, with his background in marketing, was named in 2010 as vice president and first head of a new Nike division: Nike Digital Sport.

Now with a whole Nike division devoted to Nike+ and its ecosystem, Nike has been able to turn out a number of break-through digital products in fairly short order. Among them is the Nike+ FuelBand, an electronic bracelet that measures your movements throughout the day, whether you're jogging, playing tennis, or walking between offices. The device has won raves for its elegant design and a clean interface that glows red if you've been inactive and green if you've met your daily activity goal.

"Nike has broken out of apparel and into tech, data, and services, which is so hard for any company to do," says Forrester Research analyst Sarah Rotman Epps.[30] In December 2012, Nike sealed a partnership with Techstars, a start-up mentoring firm, with the intention of wooing entrepreneurs to launch companies that will build on top of the Nike+ platform. Nike's digital ecosystem is set to grow with outside help, just like the Apple App Store and GM's App Shop. One unique feature of FuelBand is NikeFuel points, a proprietary metric of physical activity, for which Nike has already announced the development of competitive games based on racking up Fuel points.

Before Nike+, Nike was known as the world's foremost mass marketer, with a body of iconic advertising work that was matched by few other brands in the world. The unexpected success of Nike+ rapidly transformed Nike into a relationship-driven marketer, one that uses its digital services to connect directly with athletes and help them connect with and motivate each other. Nike's brand has always been about inspiring and enabling athletic performance. All that's changed is the way they do it.

It soon may be possible to classify companies only through transcendent stated missions such as Nike's. If that's the case, the entire idea of branding is set for an overhaul. The communications-centric, top-down approach of defining brands through their unique selling attributes would almost surely have to go. In its place, the strongest brands of the 21st century are destined to have clearly articulated missions that guide a wide variety of ventures within functionally integrated ecosystems of value.

Part Two

Mastering the Model

4

The Art of the Possible
Principle Four: Reimagine value creation.

For established firms in particular, applying the first three Functional Integration principles of utility, multiple contexts, and synergy can pose some significant challenges. Established companies in particular have a way of squelching even incremental innovation. Managers of all major firms are understandably invested in the products and services that helped produce their success. This is partly why so many revolutionary new digital products and services come from small start-ups. Unburdened by the responsibilities of market share and profits, start-up managers are freer to imagine, test, and try out potentially transformational ideas.

The irony is that most established companies have far greater resources to devote to research and to the development of functionally integrated digital products and services. Strong brand recognition and existing customer bases also grant such companies tremendous competitive advantages over smaller rivals in the building of ecosystems. But before any established company can enjoy these and other natural advantages through Functional Integration, that company's strategy must consciously overcome the restrictions on the imagination that success produces. Management must engage in a continual *reimagining* process concerning how the company can create, deliver, and capture value.

In order to succeed with a Functional Integration strategy, there must be a commitment to thinking and acting disruptively in order to expand the brand's digital frontiers. Digital disruption is constantly breeding new (and previously inconceivable) ways for companies to create value for their customers. Functional Integration needs to be taken on as a business model that will help you proactively engage in digital disruption. Doing so will require you to reimagine your company's activities through three specific perspectives or lenses. You must consider the opportunities that functionally integrated digital offerings might provide by looking first through a product lens, then through a brand lens, and finally through a business lens.

What does this mean in practical terms? As a very simple exercise, try reimagining the common household oven range in terms of Functional Integration. What kind of product enhancements might bring the oven range into the digital world? What if the oven controls were Wi-Fi enabled and connected to the Internet of Things? What if a mobile app or website allowed you to monitor and control remotely the temperature, timer, exhaust fan, and lighting? What if the same app could save the time and temperature settings for all your favorite recipes? Maybe an Internet-connected digital OvenCam would let you show off what's cooking via social media.

Now try to imagine what this functionally integrated oven range might do for your brand's value proposition in terms of differentiation, credibility, and relevance. Given that mobile apps and websites require registration and software updates, does the resulting relationship with customers open up marketing possibilities and increase prospects for brand loyalty? And once these customers have developed libraries of recipe settings on their smartphones, will they insist on getting your brand of oven range the next time they move? And what about marketing partnership opportunities? Would food companies want to join your oven-range platform so that they could include their recipes with automated oven settings on your app? What are the sales opportunities outside the consumer retail channel? If the Internet-connected oven range were to give your brand a special cache among younger people, is it possible to boost volume sales to rental property developers aiming at the young adult market?

Finally, try to imagine how Functional Integration might affect the future of your business as you now know it. How might the addition of the connected oven range provide your product designers and marketers with cost-free insights about your customers' cooking behaviors? Does a connected oven range enable remote diagnostics, reducing costs of repair and contributing to the engineering department's knowledge base? And might the connected oven range operate as the kitchen's digital hub? If other kitchen products could "talk" to the oven range through low-power wireless connections like Bluetooth, then all sorts of kitchen functions could be monitored and controlled through what was initially just an oven-range app. At that point, is it worth exploring making an entry into adjacent industry categories? With no single ecosystem taking ownership of the digital kitchen, perhaps it can start with your connected oven range.

Certain market realities might make the digital kitchen a tough sell. Competitive pricing pressures in the appliance market might be too great to allow such ideas to gain traction. However, it is just as likely that the same competitive pressures are making the oven market highly commoditized, pushing profits down in a race to the bottom. A few of these ideas could someday help create the kind of differentiation necessary to restore a brand's pricing power.

Even if you make and market a comparatively low-tech product like an oven range, these kinds of free-ranging questions are useful in staking out the widest possible territory for a future-oriented Functional Integration strategy. It's no accident that all the biggest and best ecosystems began modestly and developed organically over time. Consistent with the behavior of ecosystems in the natural world, ecosystems of value inevitably grow, change, and evolve in unpredictable ways. The original iTunes music library was launched only as an easy way to organize digital music and burn custom mix CDs. There was no goal of using iTunes to sell music to Apple customers. It's critical to note, however, that the iTunes platform was designed in ways that eventually allowed Apple to become the world's largest music retailer.

Functional Integration works best when you start small and stay focused on doing one thing well, while always keeping the big picture in mind. Because the ultimate goal of any Functional Integration strategy should be the creation of a complete ecosystem of value, each individual functionally integrated service should be conceived and designed to maximize possibilities for expansion and interoperability. The shape and path of each ecosystem's evolution is destined to be influenced by unknowable future variables in the form of technology, products, services, partners, and competitors. Change is the only constant with Functional Integration, which makes every ecosystem's future largely unforeseeable. Functional Integration strategies must account for this continual need to accommodate and adapt to the unknown and the unexpected.

With such a high level of uncertainty built into the business model, too much knowledge can be a threat to Functional Integration, just as it can threaten any process of business transformation. The all-too-common danger is that ideas with great transformative potential can be rejected as impractical or undesirable at their embryonic stages of development. Robert Metcalf, inventor of Ethernet and author of Metcalf's Law of telecommunications networks, predicted in 1995 that the Internet would catastrophically collapse within a year.[1] In 1981, Motorola's director of research doubted that cellphones would ever be cheap enough to displace landlines, "even if you project it beyond our lifetime."[2] In 2013, a government-sponsored survey showed that two out of five U.S. homes had *only* wireless phones, including nearly two-thirds of adults ages 25–29, and a majority of adults with incomes below the poverty level.[3]

These were men who helped found their respective industries. They knew those industries intimately. In truth, they knew so much that in these particular cases, they could hardly imagine beyond what their wealth of knowledge told them was true. That's how most of us think. On a day-to-day basis, we try to put our imaginations to work in the service of what we already know is true.

Functional Integration strategies, however, require you to steer your thinking in the opposite direction. You need to use all that you know in order to power your imagination beyond what is knowable, provable, or even possible. Specifically, you must

- Reimagine products as services
- Reimagine your brand in terms of accreted value
- Reimagine the future of the enterprise

These are not very natural ways to think inside any organization that is responsible for quarterly financial results. Imaginative thinking is generally scarce at most companies. However, within start-up firms aimed at disrupting your business model, imagination is very likely the order of the day. The people there dream about the many ways in which your profit margins might be undercut. Thinking like a disruptor helps you see your threats and opportunities for what they really are. That perspective can give you and your company a decided edge if you can somehow harness and deploy all your gifts of imagination toward the urgent task of business transformation.

○ Reimagining Products as Services

Unless you are the parent of a 10-year-old, you might be unaware of how the children's video game category has been transformed by a series called Skylanders. Introduced in October 2011, the Skylanders game Spyro's Adventure was the highest-earning children's game in North America and Europe that year[4] and the first children's video game to achieve $1 billion in sales within 15 months of its release.[5] Skylanders succeeds on the first three principles of Functional Integration: utility, multiple contexts, and synergy. It is a synergistic mash-up of contexts that delivers utility through a unique user experience.

Each Skylanders game comes packed with a starter kit of three toy action figures. Although plenty of other video games have spun off action figure collections, Skylanders action figures are different because they are the first ever to be functionally integrated with a video game. Each figure is fitted with a computer chip, so when the toy is placed on the game's "Portal of Power" accessory, a circular arena that serves as a console, its corresponding character appears on the video screen as the player's avatar. Then, as the game progresses, all the accomplishments and "level-ups" achieved through that character are saved on the action figure's computer chip, remaining available for the next game session. When a character dies too many times on screen, the player can swap it out for a new warrior.

The action figures and the Portal of Power add unique new dimensions of fun in playing Skylanders, but the chips inside the action figures also provide players with a special degree of utility. A child can take his Skylander off his PlayStation at home and go over to a friend's house and place it on an Xbox or Wii, and all the accomplishments and level-ups remain intact. Versions of Skylanders for the web, tablets, and iPhone allow the same degree of game portability across the various platforms, making Skylanders the first functionally integrated ecosystem in the video game world (Figure 4.1).

Reimagining Skylanders as something more than a traditional video game is one of those great ideas that seems obvious only after their rollout. But there was nothing obvious about the Skylanders course of development. In fact, there were plenty of excuses for never making such a game.

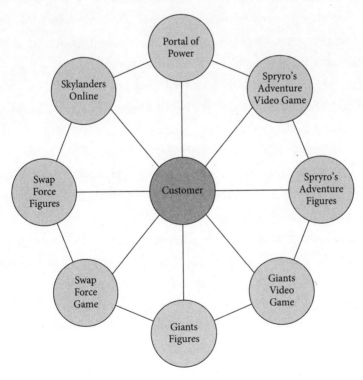

Figure 4.1 The Skylanders Ecosystem of Value

For one thing, combining computer chips and play figures was not entirely new. Webkinz, another game for small children, had been doing something similar for years. Second, there was no preexisting bond between children and the Skylanders characters, so it would have been reasonable to assume that Skylanders would have a tough time competing with games starring familiar movie characters from the Star Wars and Transformers franchises. The third problem was that the children's game market was already in decline; U.S. consumer spending on video games fell 9 percent in 2012, shortly after Spyro's Adventure was released.[6] And the fourth strike against Skylanders was that the parent company, Activision, was making its very first foray into the toy business at a time when that industry also was suffering through a down cycle. In summary, Skylanders was based on a not-that-novel concept, using untested storylines and characters and joining a gaming category in decline, while its unfamiliar action figures would also be trying to break into a flagging toy market. The Skylanders launch had disaster written all over it.

"I don't know anyone that's taken a bigger bet on a less-proven franchise based on their gut-instinct than we did with Skylanders," Activision CEO Eric Hirshberg stated in 2013.[7] In an earlier interview that same year, he'd said, "I do remember, a very short time ago, encountering a lot of people scratching their heads when we announced we were getting into the toys market…. People perceived that market to be strained; other publishers were getting out of kids' games."[8] So why did Activision move ahead anyway? Hirshberg chalks it up to magic. Activision designers regard the instant when the physical toy pops up on screen as "the magic moment."[9] Our own analysis is that the magic moment is the kind of user experience that characterizes Functional Integration. Multiple contexts, in particular, are always more interesting than single ones.

Skylanders action figures also create magic for Activision's top-line growth in the form of tremendous market synergies. An exclusive Kindle tablet version of Skylanders Cloud Patrol became the first-ever app to allow users to click through and buy Skylanders toys while playing the game. Because the action figures are sold separately in stores, Skylanders enjoys a much larger footprint than its video game competitors in Toys R Us and other toy retailers. Whereas most video games are set aside in small boxes in the gaming aisles, Skylanders is represented both in the gaming aisles *and* in big, lavish displays in the action figure aisles.

The addition of action figures also grants Activision coveted price inelasticity in marketing the Skylanders game. A Skylanders starter pack, which includes three toys and the portal, retails for about $70, which is $10 to $20 higher than the prices of competing games that don't have action figures. Another large chunk of Activision revenue comes from the more than 100 million Skylanders action figures the company has sold at about $10 each, beating out sales of action figures from such world-famous franchises as Star Wars and Transformers.

At the same time, it's important to note that most of Activision's other franchises, including its flagship Call of Duty, remain traditional video games with no functionally integrated components. And Skylanders itself still earns profits for Activision through common horizontal plays, including merchandising deals that turn out T-shirts, Halloween costumes, puzzles, and other licensed product tie-ins. Like most companies that engage Functional Integration as a new business model, Activision has moved ahead in a limited, focused way, committing to the model only where it will most likely forge a new path to growth in the company's product portfolio.

Picture a child playing pretend with his Skylanders action figures in his bedroom, then taking the toys into the living room to put them into the Portal of Power to virtually engage in a video game, and then taking them down the block to play on a friend's Skylanders system. That is a tidy snapshot of where all consumer expectations are headed. Digital disruption has turned what was a consumer products economy into an *experience* economy. Mobile communications, as we've seen, have introduced so many new contexts into people's everyday lives that consumers are increasingly craving seamless interactions with their favorite brands across the widest possible variety of interactions and touchpoints.

The ability of Functional Integration to provide seamless experiences in a wide variety of customer contexts is essential for companies to compete in the 21st century. In the case of Skylanders, Activision created a very basic digital service by outfitting action figures with computer memory so that the user's profile and game status could be shared on platforms throughout the Skylanders universe. Maintaining customer loyalty in a multicontextual digital world will require all kinds of companies to apply a similar level of imagination to their digital services as Activision did. Companies in service industries in particular, such as hotels, airlines, retailers, restaurants, and banks, should expect to be challenged by competitors offering ever faster and easier self-service through mobile communications.

At minimum, functionally integrated digital services must provide

- Practical, meaningful utility in terms of saved effort, time, and money
- Intuitive and pleasurable ease of operation
- Attractive and delightful user experiences
- Saved account settings and user histories that reward and encourage frequent repeated use
- Easy interoperability with same-brand products and services that share all of the above qualities

Reimagining products as services that deliver on all five of these criteria requires a more fluid design approach, one that embraces the ways in which customer expectations exist in a state of perpetual flux. At the reimagining stage, the earliest design stage of Functional Integration, it is important to consider many different possible futures and entire ecosystems of physical and digital objects. Such considerations are not necessarily consistent with classic product design thinking, which favors the creation of tangible, static products suitable for mass media marketing.

Reimagining products as services requires you to think holistically about user experience. Functional Integration has the word "integrity" at its root in the sense of wholeness and completeness. Customers now expect clarity and consistency from the brands they deal with. Every time they have a great digital experience with one brand, it raises their expectations for all the other brands they interact with. Failure in any one of the five criteria will only lead your customers to someone else promising to give them the seamless and satisfying digital experience they expect.

Tesco, the largest retailer in Great Britain and second largest in the world, has used Functional Integration to put itself at the forefront of digital retail innovation. Its smartphone app was among the first to allow customers to compile shopping lists by scanning household product barcodes. The shopping lists can then be moved into an online shopping basket and an order posted for home delivery. Another Tesco app tracks store loyalty points. When customers enter a Tesco store, both the shopping app and the loyalty app are automatically activated. Then the shopping app helps customers navigate the store by providing aisle numbers for all the products on their smartphone shopping lists.[10]

"Thanks to digital technology, today's customers are more powerful than ever," Tesco CEO Philip Clarke wrote in 2012. "In this multichannel world, people can now bargain hunt online, then browse in store, buy online and pick up from store."[11]

Clarke's leadership of Tesco's ecosystem has led to a company culture marked by experimentation in this kind of multicontextual shopping.

In South Korea, where 9 percent of retail sales are already transacted with smartphones, Tesco has boosted market share by creating "virtual stores" inside the Seoul subway system. Commuters waiting for their trains can scan various product barcodes from large Tesco billboards on the subway platforms. Orders made from the smartphones can be delivered and waiting for customers when they get home. Because South Koreans have so rapidly taken to smartphone shopping and home grocery delivery, digital designers there are leading the way in testing Tesco's newest concepts.

When a company like Tesco takes bold steps such as these, its purpose goes beyond competing with other supermarket chains. The barriers of entry to digital services are so low that big players like Tesco need to stay at the forefront of change and innovation. With enormous sunken investments in stores and infrastructure, Tesco and other large chains are always at risk of being victimized by more agile competitors, including start-ups that are under no short-term pressure to make profits. The only rational response to the prospects of such disruption is to use the power and wealth granted your strong market position to help inform and finance innovation. As we saw in Chapter Two, that's exactly how car companies such as Ford and BMW are taking steps to reimagine the transportation needs of the millennial generation, a generation in which 3 out of 10 haven't even bothered to get a driver's license. In the 21st century, difficult or impossible product challenges on the horizon are destined to require digital service solutions.

o Reimagining Brands as Accreted Value

Fundamentally, companies create value whenever they offer a product or service that customers will value enough to exchange for time, money, or both. That's the definition of a value equation. Technology allows for the creation of disruptive new value equations by offering customers far more value at greatly reduced costs, often through changes in context. For instance, by offering cheap online advertising as an alternative to costly classified ad listings in newspapers, Craigslist brought massive disruption to the newspaper industry's centuries-old value equation. Between 2000 and 2007, newspapers lost an estimated $5 billion worth of advertising revenue to Craigslist and other online competitors thanks to a new digital value equation that had not even existed prior to 1999.[12]

Skylanders, for instance, offered a new value equation in the children's video game category by including action figures as integral parts of the game's play design. Skylanders action figures also represented a new value equation in the toy category because their internal computer chips made them essential to the enjoyment of a video game. Taken together, the game and the action figures presented an entirely new and exciting value equation for players — and an equally exciting new business model for the sagging children's video game category. The sale of collectible action figures, which had never been a part of any video game's value equation, has added hundreds of millions of dollars in revenue to Activision's balance sheets, dollars in the toy category that the company previously had no other way of capturing.

With Functional Integration, companies willing to innovate can use these dynamics of disruption to create multiple new value equations responsible for long-term accreted value within their ecosystems. The synergistic effects inside the ecosystem proceed from a special kind of ecosystem math in which value may multiply from simple addition. Adding or upgrading just one functionally integrated piece in the ecosystem can have a multiplier effect on the ecosystem's total value equation. Nowhere is this more obvious than in Apple's and Google's app stores. Your smartphone grows in utility every time you find another appealing app to add to it or when you enjoy a free upgrade of its operating system. At that point your overall satisfaction with that ecosystem grows, ensuring you'll stick around and continue to buy products and services within that ecosystem. The synergistic value of such apps shows up in the accreted value of the respective ecosystems.

Skylanders' competitors didn't wait long to develop ecosystems of their own. In 2013 alone, no fewer than three major video game companies jumped in with rival systems. The Disney Infinity video game universe centers on an accessory that operates very much like the Skylanders Portal of Power.[13] An upgraded version of the Nintendo Wii U gamepad added NFC sensing, the same near-field communications technology as the Portal of Power. The Pokémon Rumble U game was released with NFC-enabled action figures compatible with the Wii U gamepad.[14] The Angry Birds Star Wars II video game was introduced with cheaper scanner codes instead of NFC, but the functionally integrated model of combining action figures with children's video gaming is the same.[15]

Disney Infinity action figures are drawn from hit Disney and Pixar movies, such as *Toy Story, Monsters University*, and *Pirates of the Caribbean*. Video game enthusiasts gave Disney high marks for execution, and many believe that Disney has met Activision head-on by improving the quality of the toys-to-life gaming experience. One feature in Disney Infinity called Toy Box gives children the unique ability to mash up characters from all three franchises and have them appear and compete in the same on-screen game world. But Disney Infinity is not quite as functionally integrated as Skylanders, as Disney Infinity action figures are unable to visit friends' houses with their "levels" memorized and intact.

Activision CEO Hirshberg seems to grasp Functional Integration better than Activision's rivals. "The great thing about this ecosystem is that everything talks to each other," he explained, noting the design choices Activision made in extending Skylanders to PCs, Kindles, and Apple mobile devices. "When you play on the iPhone, there are things that happen that allow you to continue to build your collection and your accomplishments between all the platforms."[16] To compete with Disney Infinity, the new Skylanders Swap Force game with an upgraded Portal of Power was released in time for the 2013 holiday season. A new array of Skylanders action figures comes in two pieces so that children can mix and match various characters' power and movement capabilities. What Hirshberg calls "dynamic swapability" allows a child to grant a Skylanders character the power of flight, for instance, by attaching the action figure to a flight-enabled base piece. In this way, the child's personal choices and actions in the physical world are made manifest in the video game, offering game players new levels of depth of involvement with Skylanders.

Prior to the arrival of Skylanders, the purchase of a children's video game was for the most part a typical one-off consumer product acquisition, not very different from buying a can of soup or a pair of running shoes. What Skylanders has brought both to its fans and to Activision is ongoing *accreted value*. Children enjoy a better, multicontextual user experience, and Activision earns more revenue. As Forbes.com game reviewer Erik Kain wrote, "Between the new Skylanders Swap Force game and toys and Disney Infinity there's really never been a better time to be a kid gamer, and never a more expensive time to be their parents."[17]

Creating mutually beneficial accretive value for both the producer and the consumer is how functionally integrated ecosystems contribute to brand building—and to overall category expansion.

Inside a healthy functionally integrated ecosystem, both user and producer share in the growth of the overall value equation. Users stand to gain more value from each connected component they add for use within the ecosystem and with each occasion on which they engage with it. The same users gain further multiples of value as each new product or service is added or enhanced over time.

Managing an ecosystem requires monitoring and adjusting this value equation periodically, always making sure that customers continue to be rewarded for using the ecosystem. The best ecosystems offer ongoing opportunities for users to deepen their involvement and enjoyment. They adhere to the principle that the more a customer puts into the ecosystem in terms of time and dollars, the more rewarding that customer's experiences within the ecosystem should become.

As a corollary, the more each ecosystem user puts in, the more the provider should benefit, as well. A successful Functional Integration strategy should focus on two specific sets of criteria that are essential to maintaining this accretive model of ecosystem management. The first set of criteria assesses the ecosystem from the perspective of value delivery to the user; the second set reflects the perspective of value capture by the producer.

Users enjoy accreted delivered value when the ecosystem

- Provides them additional utility at not much added cost
- Helps them track progress and achieve goals within the ecosystem
- Facilitates and rewards multiple purchases of ecosystem products and services

Ecosystem owners maximize accreted captured value when the ecosystem

- Gains new customers through a variety of attractive entry points
- Experiences high rates of purchases or usage per customer
- Experiences frequent repeat purchases or usage per customer
- Maintains relatively high switching costs
- Exercises pricing power above the industry average

This model of accreted value is what sets apart truly functionally integrated digital services (of which there are very few) from ordinary consumer digital services (of which there are many). Most consumer-facing digital services offer little or no accreted value at all, from either side of the value equation. Even some technically proficient and highly regarded digital services reflect instead the typical horizontal integration approach of limiting consumer contact to unrelated, unconnected two-way value exchanges. It takes Functional *Integration*, with the emphasis on integration, to achieve the full accretive power of delivering and capturing value. Table 4.1 charts the evolution of the Apple ecosystem as it has accreted value shared by both Apple and its loyal customers.

Progressive Insurance is a good example of a company that has managed to bring an accretive new value equation to one of the most heavily commoditized products in the U.S. economy: consumer auto insurance. In 2010, Progressive introduced a program in which drivers can reduce their insurance rates if they agree to install driver-behavior monitoring devices in their cars. The device, called Snapshot, fits in the palm of your hand and plugs into the standardized diagnostic port found under the driver-side dashboard of most car models.

Table 4.1   Redefining Value Through Functional Integration

Apple's functionally integrated strategy is defined by …	
Products and services …	iMac G3 desktop computer (1998)
	iBook laptop computer (1999)
	AirPort wireless base station (1999)
	iTunes (2001)
	Macintosh/OSX (2001)
	iPod (2001)
	Mac email and Internet services (2002)
	iTunes Music Store (2003)
	iPod mini (2004)
	Mac mini desktop computer (2005)
	iPod nano (2005)
	Apple TV (2006)
	Mac Book Pro (2006)
	iPhone (2007)
	App Store (2008)
	iPad (2010)
	iBookstore (2010)
	Apple Newsstand (2011)
	iCloud Internet services (2011)
	iPad Mini (2012)
	iPad Air (2013)
	iPhone 5 (2013)
that are connected …	Connectivity among devices, apps, and online services through wireless networks and the Internet.
in an ecosystem …	Data is exchanged and synchronized among devices and online services through the iTunes and iCloud platforms, creating seamless and connected experiences.
that delivers accretive value	For consumers: each generation of products and services builds on and enhances the customer experience built up from previous purchases.
	For Apple: the ecosystem enhances the value of each new product, vastly increasing the likelihood of consumer purchase and adoption.

Snapshot records such factors as miles and hours driven, sudden braking, and the hours of the day in which cars are operated. Drivers who use their cars infrequently and avoid rush-hour driving can receive significant insurance rate reductions. After 30 days of driving with the device, customers can check to see if their driving style has earned them a discount (there is no penalty if Snapshot should discover that you are a high-risk driver). If a driver then leaves Snapshot running for another six months, Progressive will use that data to recalculate a permanent renewal discount. According to a 2012 company study of five billion miles driven under the Snapshot program, 70 percent of customers receive some discount on their premiums. Discounts average $150 per year and are capped at 30 percent.[18]

In 2013, Snapshot had counted 1.4 million users in 43 states. For those users, Snapshot transformed the value equation involved with having auto insurance. In effect, Progressive customers partner with the company as active participants in risk management, a fundamental reversal of the way insurers have always operated. Snapshot offers drivers an incentive to drive less and drive more carefully, so they will have fewer accidents.[19] In fact, offering Snapshot gives Progressive a useful method for identifying its most valuable customers. Company officials say that Snapshot users stay with the company longer, reducing churn rates and the costs of acquiring new customers.[20]

Progressive's success with Snapshot can be summed up in the way it has executed on a four-step process of redefining, creating, delivering, and capturing value. Snapshot has

- Redefined value by inventing a new auto policy based on individual driving behavior
- Created value for users by offering them the same coverage benefits at reduced rates

- Delivered value through easy-to-install "set it and forget it" monitoring devices in cars
- Captured value by attracting low-risk drivers who stand to remain loyal customers due to the unique value proposition

Progressive uses Snapshot as a differentiating service that delivers accretive value over time. Once a driver has used Snapshot over a six-month period, the driver enjoys a discount that lasts as long as the driver remains with Progressive, which helps keep loyal, long-term customers. And by rewarding good driving behavior, Progressive lowers its portfolio of risk and provides a service to the community in the form of safer driving.

When coupled with its iPhone app, which gamifies incidents of hard braking and sudden accelerations, Snapshot represents the makings of a Progressive ecosystem centered on safer driving. It is a prime illustration of how Functional Integration enables companies to unlock transformative new value equations from traditional horizontally integrated product lines, as with each of the three examples shown in Table 4.2.

Improved customer data is one important by-product of this shift toward transformational value equations. Snapshot and other digital services necessarily create new data sets that can contribute accreted value for their companies. Progressive, for instance, has learned a lot about its customers and their driving habits from its

Table 4.2 Functional Integration Unlocks New Value Equations

Brand	Traditional Transactional Value Equation	Functionally Integrated Accretive Value Equation
Nike	Athletic apparel	Digital athletic empowerment
Progressive	Auto insurance	Safer driving dashboard
Skylanders	Video game	Connected toy universe

Snapshot data. The device has shown that there are on average 8 percent more cars on the road on Friday evenings, based on the number of data-calls made by Snapshot. (The data also shows that drivers spend 25 percent of their time idling in traffic and at traffic lights.) But the most important data has been produced by newer Snapshot devices that set off beeping sounds whenever drivers have "hard-braking events" to avoid collisions. Progressive has evidence that the beeping sound improves driver behavior. Says Dave Pratt, Progressive's manager of usage-based insurance, "[Our data] says people who get that kind of feedback have fewer accidents."[21]

As more and more everyday objects are embedded with sensors in the Internet of Things, marketers will increasingly gain access to previously unavailable data about how people are actually using their products. That data can then be turned back into product design or even become a core part of the product offering itself. Big data can be very expensive to obtain, but if functionally integrated services permit you to grow proprietary sets of highly detailed "owned data," that is yet another measure of the accreted value that Functional Integration offers to the brand.

o Reimagining the Future of the Enterprise

When Tesco CEO Phillip Clarke addressed a British innovation conference in November 2012, he foresaw a time in the not-so-distant future when what he calls "click and collect" will replace shopping as we know it.

"Everything from the lightbulb in your house to the car you drive will be connected to the Internet," he said. "So imagine you are leaving work, you climb into your car and order your meal for that evening and collect it at the Tesco drive-through on your way home. You won't need to tell us that you are lactose intolerant, that you want enough for your family of four, and that you don't want to exceed 800 calories per serving. We'll already know all that, and your budget. And as well as that, the lightbulb that blew in your house that morning will have added itself automatically to your Tesco order." Clarke predicted that mass personalization will affect every facet of the consumer experience, from pricing to promotions to types of products available.[22]

Tesco is second only to Walmart in global retail revenue, and operates an extensive e-commerce site as well as more than 6,000 stores in a dozen countries, including China. Tesco's emerging ecosystem of value is more ambitious in scope, if not in size, than Amazon's. It has grown to include digital book, movie, and music services. In 2013, Tesco became the first supermarket to introduce its own inexpensive Android-compatible digital tablet. With the push of a button on the tablet, Tesco's e-commerce homepage appears with a vast lineup of offerings, including banking services. Tesco's tablet embodies the idea of the supermarket reimagined as a digital service.[23]

Diligent reimagining of your products and your brand in Functional Integration terms will inevitably prompt you to consider what all these possible changes may hold for the future of your business. In the digital age, no existing business model and no single value equation is immune from attack. We have witnessed since the turn of the 21st century the demise or disintermediation of some of the largest, most successful and long-running business models at the hands of disruptive new upstarts that include Amazon, Netflix, and a blizzard of e-commerce sites too numerous to mention. Many of those employed in disrupted industries have fought in vain to retain the old ways of doing things. The music and newspaper industries come to mind in this respect. With rare exceptions, companies in these industries chose to dig in and try to protect their legacy business models rather than deploy their brand equity and market power to pursue new opportunities that might help them evolve new value equations and new business models.

Snapshot, for example, has positioned Progressive to generate any number of new possible value equations. Snapshot could monitor the driving patterns of teenagers and first-time drivers and help them learn to be safer drivers, perhaps through a digital dashboard interface. That same interface — perhaps through a Progressive app launched on Ford and GM dashboards — could work with Snapshot to recommend more efficient driving routes according to traffic and time of day. As auto insurance becomes increasingly competitive and commoditized (and with car ownership facing a downturn due to the shortage of young licensed drivers), these and other functionally integrated services might offer Progressive or any other auto insurer the prospects of new revenue streams and new ways to create, deliver, and capture value.

In order to fully reimagine the future of your business, it's important not to limit your thinking to consumer-facing services. Because all Functional Integration ecosystems inevitably generate consumer insights and user data that are relevant to your industry, ecosystems of value inevitably serve up opportunities to unlock value within each company in the form of new business-to-business ventures.

In the case of McCormick and Company, for instance, the simple tool that is FlavorPrint offers McCormick distinct opportunities to define and own the lexicon of flavor throughout the food industry, potentially embedding FlavorPrint as a de facto industry standard. From there, the possibilities for FlavorPrint and McCormick are seemingly endless.

In the short term, FlavorPrint serves as a consumer-facing service that creates value by helping consumers make more informed and satisfying recipe choices. But McCormick's greatest opportunities to monetize FlavorPrint are more likely to come through any number of potential revenue streams in the business-to-business sphere. For starters, McCormick has already formed partnerships with e-commerce websites in order to integrate FlavorPrint into the online shopping experience by recommending ingredients that go with FlavorPrint recipes.

That recommendation engine could be extended to restaurants, which might offer FlavorPrinted menus on digital tablets, so you could enter your FlavorPrint code and see which menu items you're most likely to enjoy. FlavorPrint might also be monetized through a collaborative arrangement with other food manufacturers agreeing to use FlavorPrint as a universal label on packaging. Similarly, FlavorPrint might be licensed to cooking shows and other food-related media properties.

Grocery shopping would seem to represent the most direct opportunity for FlavorPrint to grow its value equation, in part because shopping behavior is an area ripe for disruption. Studies indicate that more than 90 percent of U.S grocery shoppers prepare lists in advance of shopping and more than 70 percent never or only occasionally buy items not on those lists.[24] Once inside the store, grocery shoppers are difficult to influence. They are awash in a sea of choices, and routine buying habits tend to prevail, interrupted only by the occasional instant deal or sale item.

FlavorPrint sets out the possibility of changing these habits in partnership with the grocers. If FlavorPrint can inspire consumers to try buying new and different products because they are ingredients in FlavorPrint-recommended recipes, those new shopping habits will stand to benefit the grocery store that partners with FlavorPrint. If one store carries all the ingredients of a new FlavorPrint recipe, the shopper may alter his or her typical buying habits and make all grocery purchases in one store, altering shopping behaviors that may have previously been guided more by bargain-hunting than by convenience.

Studies show that online shoppers are particularly reliant on habit and will tend to buy repeat items with which they are already familiar. FlavorPrint has the potential to modify that dynamic by providing online shoppers with a new basis for making choices, to fulfill ingredient lists produced by FlavorPrint-recommended recipes. Online grocers might use FlavorPrint to enable shoppers to filter, sort, and search for products on the basis of their personalized FlavorPrint profiles.

It is conceivable that through this multichannel approach, FlavorPrint could lead McCormick in a transformation of the enterprise, with the FlavorPrint ecosystem conceivably expanding and graduating to the status of a functionally integrated multisided industry platform. Such a platform would enable McCormick to deliver value to consumers, grocers, distributors, media, and other food manufacturers while capturing value in multiple revenue streams from licensing, consulting, and the sale of any number of business-to-business products.

Companies with multisided industry platforms of this kind enjoy powerful benefits of network effects, made evident in the growth of software and Internet companies, including Microsoft, Intel, Cisco, Apple, Google, and Amazon. What sets such industry platforms apart from smaller ecosystems of value is that platforms also create new revenue streams for their partners in adjacent and related industry categories. Beneficiaries of Apple's platform economics include app developers, music labels, and book publishers. Amazon's platform produces revenue streams for countless manufacturers, retailers, and resellers.

One of the chief obstacles to evolving in this direction is that by reimagining your products, your brand, and your business, your thinking will likely take you beyond the capabilities of the technologies on which execution depends. The Progressive experience with Snapshot is a good example. The success of

Snapshot in 2010 was preceded by 12 years of false starts and clumsy prototypes before the technology caught up with the promise of behavior-based rate setting.

Progressive's experiments with telematics and pay-as-you-drive insurance began in 1998 with a pilot program in Houston that ran into all sorts of difficulties. At the time, it took trained technicians to install the monitoring devices and read the data. It wasn't until 2004 that Progressive was finally able to test a monitoring device that customers could install on their own. But accessing the data was still a chore, because the device had to be removed at regular intervals and connected to a PC for data upload. Only with the development of the wireless-capable Snapshot device in 2010 was Progressive able to deliver a user experience that would fulfill the goals that the company had set for consumer telematics more than a decade earlier.[25]

Giving birth to an entirely new model of auto insurance required Progressive to spend years confronting the limits of technology. But since 2010, fast-following competitors like Allstate and State Farm have copied Snapshot's business model and produced similar devices and programs, leading Progressive to sue both companies for patent infringement. Progressive may end up licensing its patents to dozens of other insurers—which, on the upside, would create a new business-to-business revenue stream. The drawback is that licensing would erode Progressive's hard-won brand differentiation, challenging Progressive to continue to experiment, innovate, and push the boundaries of its enterprise further still.[26]

True to its name, Progressive has always had something of a forward-thinking, challenger mind-set. It was the first major auto insurance company to open a website (1995) and the first to offer instant insurance quotes online (1996).[27] It takes strong leadership to achieve such results in the face of early innovative flops and failures. Many CEOs give mixed signals as to whether they are ready to be disruptors before they can be disrupted. The IBM 2012 Global CEO survey showed that more than 70 percent of them insist on the importance of developing new business models.[28] But existing business models are more often considered sacred components of corporate strategy. It takes discipline to engage a new business model at the expense of one that is proven, battle-hardened—and ripe for disruption.

○   ○   ○

Too often, leaders of enterprises will fight to protect and defend certain business models long after their potential for growth has been exhausted. However, when business models are seen as flexible, dynamic, and subject to change over time, they empower the people within the enterprise to step back from legacy products and projects to unleash new potential into the market. They can find new multisided, functionally integrated opportunities to create widely diversified revenue streams as hedges against future disruption. Then, current products and business models can serve as beacons that light the path to the future instead of fortresses that defend the past.

5

The Digital Service Launchpad

Principle Five: Redesign value delivery.

Each of the companies that lead the way in Functional Integration—Amazon, Apple, Google, and Nike—has a clear brand purpose, one that resonates with consumers and is reflected by its ecosystem. Amazon stands for customer-centric shopping. Apple stands for exceptional computing experiences. Google stands for organizing the world's information. Nike stands for outstanding athletic performance. All four of these companies have used their respective brand purposes to inform the design decisions necessary to deliver on the first four principles of Functional Integration. In order to contribute to the creation of value through utility, multiple contexts, and synergy, each new piece or capability added to their ecosystems must deliver value in ways that embody the brand purpose.

When Steve Jobs initially hesitated to develop iTunes software for PC-compatible computers, he was making a conscious choice to hold back delivery of value to PC owners in favor of trying to induce them to buy Macintosh computers. Jobs' recalcitrance at that time only made sense if the purpose of his company (then known as Apple Computers) was to sell more computers. Opening iTunes to a competing operating system, in contrast, was more aligned with the brand purpose, and that's what Apple ended up doing. It turned out to be the smarter business decision, because it delivered value to the other 95 percent of computer users who previously had no access to Apple's functionally integrated ecosystem.

This fundamental question of purpose is the primary challenge that every horizontally integrated company faces when making its initial venture into Functional Integration. If L'Oreal Paris's sole purpose had been selling more beauty products instead of "the universalization of beauty," there would be no My Signature Beauty. If Progressive's sole purpose had been providing cheaper car insurance, it would not have invested a dozen years in the development of Snapshot.

There is much more than semantics involved in a discussion of brand purpose. It is absolutely crucial to the development of an ecosystem that brand purpose is understandable to employees and consumers alike. A horizontally integrated company that has been getting by without a brand purpose (beyond making money and moving products) will likely fail at Functional Integration unless it discovers or develops a purpose that will resonate with consumers. In the absence of that resonance, consumers are unlikely to perceive the utility of partaking in the company's ecosystem.

A company's brand purpose does not have to be grand or idealistic in order to succeed with Functional Integration. It only has to be appealing and easily understood. Amazon's purpose is not so different from that of the British retailer Tesco, which has a well-developed ecosystem of value based on the brand purpose of bringing "the best value, choice and service to our millions of customers each week." In 2013, Target's ecosystem added a digital video service called Target Ticket, which clearly reflects the Target ethos of "expect more, pay less." Distinct from Apple's and Amazon's video stores, Target Ticket prominently displays bargain-priced collections of 99-cent rentals, weekly deals, and 50-percent-off videos, all redolent of Target's discount retail pricing tactics. The Target site also reflects the retailer's family focus by offering children's videos classified in six different age ranges, from preschool to teen.[1]

The design of Target Ticket's homepage is clean and free of clutter, which serves as a reminder that good design always involves important questions about what the product is *not* and which features *not* to include. This is especially true in the design of a simple functionally integrated digital service, such as a mobile app, because any disappointment in the user's experience can result in quick rejection by that user.

Designers commonly draw a distinction between usefulness and usability, but with digital products and services, each one has an exceptionally strong effect on the other. The primary Functional Integration principle of utility will suffer if a useful service is difficult to use or if an easy-to-use service proves to be of little useful value. Poorly designed products and services are often so overloaded with features that their user interfaces are cluttered and confusing. Usefulness and usability both suffer, but the number of such poor designs will likely continue to grow, because it takes an exceptional level of disciplined focus on brand purpose to save such a product or service from getting overstuffed with bright ideas.

In the design stage of the Nike+ FuelBand, for instance, there was no shortage of great ideas about the types of utility the wristband fitness tracker could provide for its users. The FuelBand's sensors were capable of much more than measuring casual, daily activity, which was the original idea behind FuelBand's development. The sensors could also monitor heart rate, measure galvanic skin response (an indicator of emotional states), and tell users how well they had slept that night.[2]

Because the FuelBand was conceived as a functionally integrated piece of the Nike+ ecosystem, adding capabilities to each member's account offered another set of tempting options. Perhaps FuelBand wearers could earn points that would be integrated with charitable running events or earn cash credits toward Nike products. Syncing the FuelBand with Nike+ would also allow Nike to control the LED lighting on the FuelBand, so that at special moments, such as the start of the Olympics, all the FuelBands in the world could light up at once.[3]

These were all interesting ideas that failed to make it into the FuelBand launch in 2011. One concern was that each additional feature adds complexity, and complexity can cause problems with digital products. Nike products, which are dedicated to enhancing athletic performance, can't afford to have performance issues of their own. When performance is part of the brand mission, that sets an especially high bar for performance of the ecosystem.

But the chief consideration in such product development decisions was Nike's brand purpose. In the development process preceding the launch of FuelBand, Nike vice president Stefan Olander was able to edit the FuelBand's features down to that essence of brand purpose. Olander determined that FuelBand buyers are interested foremost in enhancing their athletic performance. They want to quantify their activity today and use that metric to summon the motivation to do better tomorrow. And when they hit their new goals tomorrow, they want to hear the FuelBand beep and watch its green LEDs light up as a reward. Any features that didn't contribute to those user goals were left on the drawing table. Monitoring of heart rate and sleep activity and earning free gear were all considered beside the point at the time. For FuelBand to succeed as a functionally integrated product in

Nike's ecosystem of value, it meant that its *functions* had to be *integral* to the Nike brand.

When the iPod was first introduced, it faced a lot of criticism for what it was unable to do. The rechargeable battery couldn't be swapped out. Memory couldn't be added. The iPod was deliberately designed to have fewer features than other digital music players available at the time, because fewer features made the computer experience simpler and more enjoyable, consistent with Apple's brand purpose. When the iPod proved to be a hit, Apple was lauded for the device's simple, attractive design and ease of use, but these attributes were the result of the iPod's being one part of a functionally integrated ecosystem. Thanks to the synergies of its ecosystem, the iPod maintained a distinctive design focus that helped it set the bar for portable music.

Products from horizontally integrated companies are often weighed down with features that set them apart from functionally integrated competitors. Complexity for the sake of adding lots of different capabilities reflects the lack of a higher purpose in the brand. Design considerations are less important because horizontally integrated companies rely on traditional marketing and advertising to create demand for the product, and advertising typically puts product utility last as a consideration.

To develop a product or service for Functional Integration, we begin with what's most interesting. Outside the mass media context of interruption, being interesting is the first and only thing that matters in terms of delivering value to the user. Once there is initial user engagement, attracted by the quality of being interesting, then the user is able to infer through interaction with the ecosystem the relevant messages about the brand. What consumers know about Apple, Amazon, Google, and Nike they learn firsthand through these brands' products and services. This dynamic creates a depth of connection with these brands that can't be matched through interruptive advertising messages.

It takes disciplined decision making to ensure that digital designs in particular fulfill the purposes of being interesting, delivering value, *and* delivering on the brand purpose. Achieving this effect in launching even the most modest functionally integrated service presents a new range of choices, which fall under four broad areas of execution:

- Territories
- Technology
- Talent
- Teamwork

Companies need to equip and prepare the organization for Functional Integration by making crucial decisions about the strategies they choose for breaking into adjacent industries, the types of technology innovation they will pursue, the types of people needed to deliver digital services, and the new methods of planning and production required to bring an ecosystem to market.

o Stake Out a New Territory

When functionally integrated companies move into new consumer territories, the moves are rarely made in pursuit of immediate direct profit, but more likely because the company's ecosystem opened a new area to build accretive value. Competitors and industry watchers, bound by horizontal integration thinking, often greet such moves with surprise and underestimate the newcomer's chances of success. Toy industry experts openly questioned Activision's choice to enter their space. Microsoft's then-CEO Steve Ballmer famously claimed in 2007 that "there's no chance that the iPhone is going to get any significant market share. No chance."[4] Amazon's creation of the Kindle that same year seemed foolhardy because Sony—the world's greatest electronics maker—had struggled for years in that space.

Industry gossips had predicted disaster for the Kindle all through the three years that Amazon's digital reader had been under development. Then the new Kindle sold out almost instantly after its release. No one appreciated how the Kindle is not really a device at all, that Bezos and his Amazon team managed to reimagine the product as a service. "Once you add that wireless radio and put a store on the device it's really not a device anymore," Bezos explained at the time. He admitted, however, that he would still refer to the Kindle as a device, just to avoid confusion: "If you call it a device people know what you mean and if you call it a service they don't. A disconnected device is really a device. This is not."[5] So Kindle buyers were invited to miss the distinction. They simply gave the Kindle high marks for its ease of use. Although it appeared from a horizontal integration viewpoint that Amazon had invaded a new territory, in fact it had expanded its existing ecosystem of value by offering a new functionally integrated service—disguised as a device.

Apple's opening of the iTunes store was a lot like Amazon's introduction of the Kindle. Both were territorial expansions that, through Functional Integration, instantly increased the accreted value of their respective existing ecosystems. Thanks to their growing ecosystems, entering these new territories made sense in terms of customer needs, rather than on the basis of category-bound prospects for profit. Target's digital video service and Tesco's proprietary digital tablet are both ecosystem extensions that employ the same logic. They are plays for long-term accretive value, rather than horizontally integrated bids for profitable new product lines.

Entering adjacent territories is an essential task for most horizontally integrated companies that want to use Functional Integration to embody their corporate purpose. Most companies, however, limit the expression of their purpose to marketing campaigns. Coca-Cola is a case in point.

Coca-Cola's stated mission is "To refresh the world. To inspire moments of optimism and happiness. To create value and make a difference."[6] Since 2009, Coca-Cola has marketed itself with a global campaign based on this mission, a campaign called Open Happiness. Company officials even say that Coke is determined to "own" the territory of happiness.[7] But Coke has pursued happiness mainly through media-friendly, attention-getting Open Happiness events. Coke has orchestrated such publicity stunts as deploying a Hug Machine in Singapore and a Happiness Machine in New York that dispensed flowers and pizza.[8]

Coca-Cola claims that it has employed scientists and economists to study happiness, which is not so different from L'Oreal Paris's scientific studies of beauty or Nike's studies of athletic performance. The difference is that those companies have used their expertise to develop multicontextual digital tools that hold people's interest and help them understand themselves. Coke, in contrast, has used its knowledge of happiness in the context of interruption, with stunts that are about Coke, not its customers. What Coke has yet to do is create digital tools for happiness that transcend mere moments in time. An ecosystem of value, based on the brand purpose of happiness, might provide customers with ways to "open happiness" beyond opening a beverage can.

Coke's experts have defined common sources of happiness as being together, being active, being in the moment, being curious, and giving. Developing an ecosystem of value around such a brand purpose might lead Coca-Cola to diversify its activities into territories more easily supported by Functional Integration, such as entertainment venues for families. By diversifying the company's offerings away from its hundreds of horizontally integrated lines of products, and in line with its stated brand purpose, Coca-Cola could start to build an ecosystem of value — and sell more beverages, too.

o Deliver Innovation Through Technology

Functional Integration requires innovating with technology, but it does not depend on technological innovation. You want to deliver value in innovative ways *through* technology, but success in delivering value rarely relies on making technological breakthroughs. In order to create a product or service that offers utility in multiple contexts and in ways that promise synergies for your ecosystem, all the technology you need probably already exists.

Consider the abundance of innovation available to any company through the technology available on the internet. Yet most brands devote their attention to using this sophisticated technology as a delivery mechanism for content. Marketers spend billions yearly on digital content, in the mistaken belief that the web is yet another new channel of mass media. But the web, with its multiple contexts, is in truth an escape from the single context of mass media. Occasionally some piece of content such as a viral video attracts a significant viewership, but even in those circumstances, the value such a video creates (for the viewer or the brand) is ephemeral. In a multicontextual digital environment, there can be no lasting value creation without utility.

Cars were once called "horseless carriages," because understanding the context of transportation at the time was limited to that of horses and carriages. For the same reason, early radios were called "wireless sets." In a similar way, Functional Integration is a useful term today because it distinguishes itself from the dominant contexts of business models involving digital content, which are neither functional nor integrated.

Marketers who fail to consider the importance of multiple contexts in the new digital age tend to see apps and websites as though they constitute yet another category of media. They deploy online content similarly to the way they deploy content in all media, in the form of text and videos to lure visitors to a branded website. Their hope is that by association, the content will inform and entertain long enough through the context of interruption to deliver the brand message. Used in this way, digital content is all about the brand. No different from all other advertising, digital media are used as a channel for the brand to tell consumers about itself.

But that approach is directly at odds with the expectations of consumers who are acclimated to a multicontextual digital environment. Today's consumers expect brands to help them know and understand themselves. The best functionally integrated products and services are about the people who use them, not about the brands they represent. A good digital service provides its user with meaningful, personalized value, which motivates the user to rely on it regularly. The brand captures value only through the development of each user's personal engagement with the service. Online content and advertising try to get consumers to know the brand better, which utterly fails the first test of being interesting. Consumers are interested in themselves first and foremost, and well-conceived digital services help them cultivate knowledge of themselves *through* the brand.

It's very easy to mistake content as a service because online content is descended from newspaper and magazine writing, and in the predigital analog-only world, articles that offered tips and advice were often called "service pieces." But service means something else entirely in the digital world. Online content doesn't qualify as a service because content does not directly involve the user in an ongoing relationship. A typical magazine "service piece," for instance, might offer general tips on applying makeup. My Signature Beauty, by contrast, is a digital service that offers specific makeup suggestions that are best suited to you.

Functionally integrated digital services and products allow for personalization and access to communities of people engaged on the same basis. Communities form around people, not content. Facebook and Twitter, for instance, produce no content at all. People form communities at these sites because the sites afford access to other people with similar interests and passions. The 21 million members of the Nike+ community have been brought together by the tools that Nike+ has provided and not simply because they are interested in Nike. It's because Nike has offered them tools that are interesting. Their personalized Nike+ data helps them become better athletes, and that shared experience prompts them to participate in Nike's community of athletes.

So what makes a functionally integrated service interesting? We have found that some of the most useful and personalized functionally integrated services can be derived from just three innovative applications of data based technologies:

- **Metrics** allow people to quantify and track their personal behavior in order to inspire and maintain behavioral change. The Nike+ ecosystem is dedicated to providing athletes with metrics for running and other activities, while producing ongoing progress in metrics for other sports.
- **Algorithms** help people make faster and better decisions by narrowing their range of choices on the basis of past decisions. Netflix is a fine example of how a digital tool can make movie recommendations, just by estimating the behavior of people whose movie rental history most closely resembles your own. McCormick FlavorPrint uses algorithms in a different way, but for the same purpose, to help customers make better decisions.
- **Visualization** helps make metrics and algorithms easier for people to understand and utilize. Charts and heat maps

can make trends in performance metrics clearer, providing more immediate motivation to change. L'Oreal Paris's My Signature Beauty employs all three of these technologies, but it is visualization that helps each of its users understand her personal makeup needs more fully.

The application of these technologies is responsible for the functionally integrated personalized and customized services that had been unavailable to consumers prior to the digital revolution. Innovation in these services, however, is not found within the technologies themselves but within their application. Relatively simple data tools based on these technologies provide gateways into functionally integrated ecosystems because the resulting personalized services are interesting enough and provide enough utility that users will take the trouble to register. Without a sufficiently useful digital service that is all about the user, you are unlikely to gain registrations. And without registrations, there is no ecosystem.

Digital services built on metrics, algorithms, and visualizations are so compelling that they can build large followings despite their limitations. All diet-related apps, for example, provide only general estimations for food calorie counts, as it is impossible to chemically analyze the caloric value of the actual food you eat. Motion-sensing devices like the Nike FuelBand are prone to some inaccuracy in their metrics, but their tracking capabilities still provide an enormous motivation for people who want to stick to their exercise regimes. Amazon's and Apple's e-book stores have yet to produce book graphics that are as attractive and reliable as the ones found on the printed page. In each of these cases, the utility provided by these digital tools outweighs their limitations.

Some of these problems might be overcome through actual technological innovation, but taking that path runs the risk of disappointing users. A reliable mash-up of existing technologies can be much more satisfying to the customer than a technological breakthrough with a poor user interface. With digital services, you get no points from consumers for originality if your technical breakthrough can't deliver actual utility and an excellent user experience.

o Fill the Gaps in Talent

Prospective clients regularly approach digital agencies and consultancies such as R/GA with the misperception that making digital products is not so different from making websites or online videos. Marketers accustomed to outsourcing advertising work to outside agencies tend to expect that all digital work can be similarly outsourced to digital agencies.

The hands-off client may be a dream client for most firms, but Functional Integration requires client engagement in order to succeed. From our perspective, the client company needs people with strong points of view about what the company wants for its customers, and some digital training and expertise to understand how to champion their digital ambitions. In our experience, at least one or two people from the client's side should have some experience building a consumer-facing digital service, even if that service is just a plain vanilla e-commerce site. Even better is a client with someone on board who has worked for a software or digital platform company or has been part of a digital start-up. Having at least one person with some digital expertise in the field can pay for itself many times over. Without such experience, you risk going down too many blind alleys and taking too many wrong turns—mistakes you wind up paying for in lost time and added expenses. Someone on the client team needs to be making informed decisions throughout the process. This person needs to know the company's priorities and be able to interpret them in

Functional Integration terms, stressing the importance of utility and user experience. It is a critical role that cannot be outsourced.

In helping clients equip their organizations for digital capabilities, we have learned how difficult it can be to attract top-notch digital talent. Companies must convince prospective digital hirees that the companies are committed to digital transformation. Job seekers need to see the vision and understand that they will be empowered to deliver it. Attracting digital talent also requires you to protect them from corporate bureaucracy, because digital workers thrive in fast-moving entrepreneurial environments. Finally, you must show that you have the funding and other resources necessary to deliver on the vision. The best digital talent is in high demand. They can afford to be picky about where they want to go, and that decision is usually based on where they feel they will be most supported.

Most corporate teams assigned to build digital services are heavily influenced by both the marketing department (people who know consumers but not necessarily technology) and the information technology department (people who know technology but not necessarily the consumer). Functional Integration requires a merger of both disciplines to some extent, which means that the process in some circumstances can be plagued with talent-related pitfalls.

A 2013 report from Accenture points to serious areas of disconnect between chief marketing officers and chief information officers. Accenture found, for instance, that almost half of all CMOs would like their employees to access data and digital content without the help of the CIO's staff, while nearly half of all CIOs complain that CMOs bring in outside technologies with little regard for internal IT standards. The survey also found that CMOs and CIOs are generally disinclined to work together. CIOs say that their most important C-suite relationship is with the corporate head of finance, while CMOs say that their most important ally is the head of sales. They also tend not to agree on priorities. CIOs see data primarily as a source of marketing campaign optimization, while CMOs want data to generate leads and sales.

All these disconnects contribute to this finding: only one out of four CIOs and CMOs says that his or her company has integrated data for both online and offline customers. Four out of ten are struggling with this issue. The Accenture report recommends that a CMO for the digital age needs to be regarded as the chief experience officer, or CXO, with the IT department operating as a strategic partner instead of a platform provider.[9]

In our view, the Accenture report explains the need for building internal talent around Functional Integration capabilities. At a minimum, any company looking to develop a functionally integrated ecosystem must involve two key executives in its development. One, most likely from a marketing background, is needed to represent strategy, as a vice president of digital product strategy. The other, coming from a technology background, should look after the technical and operational road map, as vice president of digital product development. Avoiding terms such as "marketing" and "technology" in their titles is deliberate. The fusion of marketing with technology in the development of digital products and services means that distinguishing the two is not always helpful.

If staffing up for Functional Integration seems a little outside the box, consider that companies didn't always hire marketing professionals to work with advertisers. Marketers joined the C-suites as it became increasingly important for every major company to master the discipline of horizontal integration. The same story played out later with vertical integration. There had never been a need for chief information officers until the demands of automation made it necessary to hire professionals to streamline and optimize company data. Hardly any companies currently have the requisite talent to do their own digital service design, but companies that want to grow ecosystems of digital products and services in the coming years should consider beginning to staff up in that direction. The chronic inability of CMOs and CIOs to integrate their multichannel databases points to a rising pressure for these in-house capabilities to become functionally integrated.

In order to achieve such a goal, it is vital to project an organizational vision for the future of digital services. If you have aspirations of creating new business models and generating new revenue streams from digital services, then you will need to manage and support digital services as you would any other product offering, with R&D, product strategy, product development, brand management, and customer service.

But first you will need to chart a road map for ecosystem governance that is right for your culture and can scale to your ultimate ambitions. In your current state, it is likely that you have people responsible for "digital" in three places that are probably overlapping: marketing, IT, and digital. Digital usually sits inside of marketing or IT, unless there is an e-commerce team that sits within sales or channels.

The primary initial to-do items are

1. **Sort out your digital talent**. Who do you have who can create digital services? Digital media and digital advertising talent are not what you're looking for. You need people who can design and develop digital services (like mobile apps, self-service kiosks, video games) — people like software engineers and user experience experts. Your existing digital talent pool may run only as deep as your website team.
2. **Give digital services a home**. Determine the future home for running digital services as though it were a start-up business within the company. All the foundational principles of the "lean start-up" movement and agile software development

apply to the creation of digital products and services, including such concepts as rapid prototyping, the minimally viable product, and using quantifiable data to inform the process of continuous development.

After these two steps have been taken, staffing the digital unit can become more focused because job descriptions for new positions can be written to ensure proper alignment of roles and responsibilities with organizational positioning. Hiring in an area that is poised for such rapid growth and change challenges you to take stock of your digital ambitions and assess how gaps in talent and capabilities might prove to be obstacles a year or two after a hire is made. At R/GA it is so important to mesh talent choices with the future direction of our clients' digital services that we developed a set of recruitment services to complement the clients' own hiring functions. In working so closely with clients, we find it makes sense in some cases for us to play a strong role in the interviewing, vetting, and onboarding of new digital talent—people on whom our future work together relies.

One thing to keep in mind with regard to talent is that talent outside your doors can be a big contributor to your success with Functional Integration. Thanks to open API (application platform interface) architecture, third-party outside developers can create new apps and software products using certain data from your platform to contribute to your ecosystem.

These third-party developers use APIs to operate as informal testers of new ideas, products, and territories, offering lessons for ecosystem owners at little or no risk to the owners. Apple, for instance, has repeatedly drawn inspiration and insights from popular third-party apps inside its ecosystem and then developed its own proprietary apps to capture more value for itself (most prominently by replacing Google Maps with its own maps app). In this way, APIs can perform some of the "bleeding edge" experimentation that companies often pay their staffs to perform. We will cover APIs more extensively in Chapter Seven, but they are worth a mention here for the way in which they can contribute to and extend the reach of your digital talent's capabilities.

o Embrace Agile Teamwork

As a new type of business model, Functional Integration requires new forms of teamwork. Built from our experience, we have developed a synchronous design process to help us deliver on digital products and services in ways that design and production meant for horizontally integrated product lines never could.

With synchronous design, we perform fast, multiple iterations of product and service prototypes using multidisciplinary teams working in parallel with each other (Figure 5.1). Team members from diverse perspectives and roles confront common problems and challenges in three stages or cycles called Explore, Experiment, and Execute. At each stage, teams challenge or reexamine the going-in hypotheses (a process we call "flaring") and then eliminate or disprove hypotheses (a process we call "focusing").

In the Explore cycle, the design group begins by investigating product or service possibilities in order to arrive at a set of ideas that are supported by a consumer need or pain point. (Those ideas must contribute to a viable business model opportunity that is aligned with brand strategy.) Then the group uses prototyping and consumer feedback in the Experiment cycle to test the ideas. In the final cycle, Execute, the group develops a cohesive proposed design solution, based on a minimum viable product or service offering.

The synchronous design process might begin with a product brief to transform a stand-alone home appliance into a smart connected device that offers valuable new services because the appliance knows something about the user and the user's lifestyle.

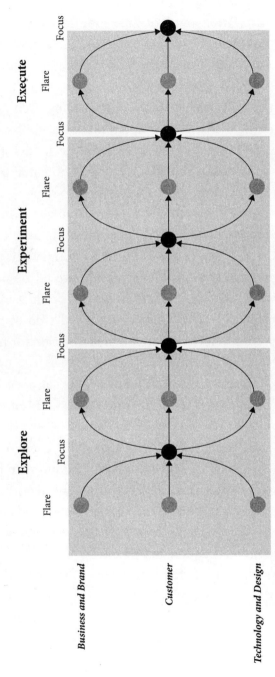

Figure 5.1 R/GA Synchronous Design Process

The ultimate ambition may be for this new appliance to become a source of daily inspiration and motivation for the user, beyond its functional purpose. Arriving at a solution for such a brief requires coordinating work around four activities: product design, service design, business modeling, and brand strategy.

A traditional approach would call for tackling each of these four activities sequentially. The company would begin by spending months identifying and sizing up the business model strategy. Then it would spend more months arriving at potential product design options. Devising the optimal brand strategy would consume additional months, in order to determine how the product and related services would fit into the company's existing product portfolio and brand architecture, along with pricing and distribution strategies. The final months would be devoted to creating services or software to support the product offering. This is the typical 18-month-long "product-led" "go-to-market process" that has characterized horizontal integration for most of the past century.

Synchronous design tackles all four activities at once in that three-cycle Explore, Experiment, Execute process. This approach enables companies to get their ideas to market faster, while also revealing potential weaknesses in strategy early enough in the design process that they can be addressed. The ultimate benefit of synchronous design is that the interchange of ideas between and among the various disciplines produces a better end product, bringing concepts and approaches to light that would never have arisen in the traditional sequential process.

The Explore phase is staffed with teams of experts who represent all four strategic disciplines: business, product, brand, and services. Each project has a single leader to orchestrate the process across all four activities, but each discipline is charged with solving its own respective piece of the puzzle, in consultation with the other teams.

In one such case of designing a Wi-Fi–enabled home appliance, the business modeling team began by exploring options for different business models at a conceptual level—direct to consumer, business to business, subscription models, freemium services, and others. Meanwhile, the brand strategy team used online focus groups and survey research to investigate options for brand positioning as a lifestyle choice, a design choice, and an environmentally conscious choice. The product design team assessed different form factors for the machine, trying out various sizes, shapes, and combinations of features. The service design team in the meantime studied the abundance of digital services that could be delivered through the machine itself, as well as through smartphones, tablets, and laptops.

After each of these teams had time to flare and explore their respective pieces of the design problem, they reconnected at predetermined collaboration points during which they shared with each other their work in progress. The various teams then had opportunities to challenge and debate each other, trying out their hypotheses and testing their ideas, which triggered the focus phase of the Explore stage. The focus phase forced the members of these disparate fields of expertise to connect their puzzle pieces, enabling them to sharpen their thinking, address their weakness, or pivot in new directions based on what they'd learned from each other. Each of these collaboration points help create shared ownership and accountability, with the shared assumption that the product's end user is the ultimate boss.

Moving on to the Experiment cycle enabled each of the four teams to identify serious weaknesses and alternative solutions before making any big decisions affecting development of the Wi-Fi appliance. The business modeling team prepared a set of prototypes of revenue models, while the brand strategy team created proposed brand concepts, including language and imagery. The product design team developed a range of machine prototypes, some as physical mock-ups and others in computer renderings. The service design team developed prototypes of the most instrumental service experiences, including mobile apps.

In the final focus phase of the Execution cycle, the entire design group came together with

- An operational business model, supported by a financial model
- Recommendations for brand positioning, language, and identity
- Detailed design renderings and specifications
- User experience/interface design requirements, data dependencies, and technical requirements

These final deliverables, produced in less than half the time required for traditional product development, included all the specifications and other information needed to start production. The resulting prototypes and video demonstrations were designed to gain buy-in for the new product throughout the organization.

Synchronous design relies on customer observation and interaction throughout the process. A design group will continually form and assess hypotheses through *in situ* research methods, such as ethnography and contextual inquiry, in order to understand consumer needs and pain points surrounding product and service touchpoints. The group attempts to gauge reactions to our concepts from real people in the context of their actual lives. Rather than conducting focus groups in artificial environments, designers will send prototypes to people to use at home or work. As the saying goes, to understand the lion, visit the jungle, not the zoo.

Conducting this kind of process at scale may require us to assemble communities of carefully chosen participants who will engage with us over a period of several weeks or months. We might recruit a group of 250 people spread across nine countries that are strategically important to our client. Then, in order to home in on the underlying reasons why a product or service concept is not resonating with those 250 participants, we will conduct contextual inquiries in the homes of perhaps 24 of them, in three or four different cities.

From the perspective of someone accustomed to sequential product and service development processes, the synchronous design process can appear overwhelming and chaotic. Clients who have made their careers in horizontally integrated businesses are often baffled by some of these practices and procedures. The process invites heartfelt debate and episodes of intense collaboration. Daily stand-up check-ins among team members are common, rather than weekly or semimonthly updates. Synchronous design is a process that encourages taking leaps of faith to discover breakthroughs, rather than settling for the least common denominator by making incremental tweaks.

One frequent objection to synchronous design involves the intense usage of staff time. Company officials looking to cut costs will sometimes ask, "Why does it require so many people to get to the answer?" Our response is that synchronous design is aimed at getting things right faster, the first time around. Traditional design, with its long lead times and slow pacing, might appear to represent a more efficient allocation of resources, but it is also more likely to result in do-overs and lost time to market.

To help those who are unfamiliar with this iterative and multidisciplinary approach to teamwork, here are our top five lessons learned for conducting synchronous design:

1. Synchronous design is not done in a black box. Client partners need to be hands-on with the process. Firsthand exposure to customers is incredibly valuable. It makes the research tangible and facilitates a common understanding of design issues and opportunities.

2. Make sure all key stakeholders are on the same page before beginning the process. All parties must be clear about the uses and outcomes of the qualitative research process as well as its limitations. It's also critical to establish a process for regularly managing expectations around input, feedback, and documentation.

3. Immortalize key customer quotes to keep a living record of insights that led to breakthrough understanding. Display them prominently.

4. Expose each discipline to firsthand observation. For instance, don't sequester customer knowledge within the brand strategy team. Each discipline contributes unique viewpoints to the body of shared learning. Those multiple viewpoints are important in subsequent collaborations.

5. Document the logic behind decisions. The synchronous design process moves so quickly that stakeholders who aren't involved on a day-to-day basis can get anxious about what may appear to be sudden, inexplicable changes. Be prepared to offer executives a simplified, high-level overview of how and why certain design choices were made.

Clients who are anxious to achieve a final result are not always comfortable with this process. They often want to "make" an ecosystem instead of growing one over time. We have learned the hard way that functionally integrated services shouldn't try to do too much on their first launch. Past attempts at launching ecosystems in an all-at-once approach — what might be called trying to boil the ocean — persuaded us that we learn more and reduce risk by launching one service at a time and taking turns to see how each one is put to use before refining it further.

The downside of this approach is that return on investment can be difficult to foresee. The accretive value of a long-term commitment to Functional Integration is not so obvious when the client is looking at an attractive but modest first effort at a digital service. Sometimes we find it useful to count up all the future accretive value that one single part of a future functionally integrated ecosystem might represent. Reimagining value and reimagining the brand as accretive value are ongoing processes.

Synchronous design can be very helpful in producing digital products and services in short, six- to nine-month development periods. A new digital service should be a "minimally viable" product, one that is simple enough to understand immediately, but one that also offers enough meaningful utility to be "sticky" and attract repeat visits. After launch, the process of monitoring and tracking customer usage, which is covered in the following chapter, is the only way to really learn about what you've accomplished.

o o o

None of today's largest and most important ecosystems of value were ever planned much beyond a three-year horizon, because planning farther ahead is neither possible nor desirable. The development of every digital service, platform, and ecosystem constitutes a figurative journey, which is why all software development is managed with road maps that document the features to be added and fixes to be made in subsequent versions. As with ecosystems in the natural world, ecosystems of value develop over time, and often in ways that are hard to predict. That's the best case to be made for designing fast, putting a product out there, and iterating quickly.

6

The Drivers of Connected Growth

Principle Six: Redirect toward value capture.

When Larry Page and Sergei Brin launched Google in the late 1990s, they did so without a business model, mainly because the Google search engine had been created as an academic exercise. Once Google received venture funding in 1999, adding banner advertising to the site would have been a natural next step, in order to raise revenue and fund Google's growth. The speed and accuracy of Google searches was attracting so much web traffic that Google would have been an attractive destination for advertisers.

Google's founders, however, resisted. Their first objection was that banner ads would compromise the user experience by increasing the time it took for each search page to load and render. Second, Brin said, "the ad has nothing to do with the search. Why would we show it? It's distracting."[1] Right from the start, the duo who would later turn the digital age context of "search" into a $300 billion juggernaut was dismissive of the traditional advertising context of interruption.

The Google ecosystem developed in subsequent years with a similar focus on user utility. Acquisitions such as Usenet, Blogger, Picasa photo sharing, and Keyhole satellite mapping were undertaken in order to help speed searches of these sites, as Google-owned resources were easier to index than other sites.

The introduction of Gmail in 2004 marked the first time that Google used the ecosystem's synergy to create a new value proposition for registered Google members. Because its search engine required massive amounts of cheap computer memory, Google's Gmail offered 1,000 megabytes of free email storage at a time when other free webmail services, such as Microsoft and Yahoo, could offer only 10 megabytes. In addition, Gmail's search function, because it also was Google run, worked far better than that of rival webmail services.

With the later development of the Google Chrome web browser and operating system, and with Google's entry into mobile communications through Android, the Google Play app store, and its purchase of Motorola's mobile phone business, the growth of Google's functionally integrated ecosystem has moved continually between adding functions and expanding integration. Google continues to innovate with new functional points for entering its ecosystem (as with Google Glass, the wearable mobile device) and with its January 2014 purchase of Nest Labs, the maker of high-tech thermostats and smokes alarms, widely considered to be potential hubs for web-connected appliances.[2]

Technology and data, as in the Google example, are like sunlight and water to a growing ecosystem. As the name Functional Integration implies, ecosystems grow in terms of function (adding value to the ecosystem) and integration (adding connections within the ecosystem). The challenge is to use insights drawn from new technologies and data analysis to inform growth in both of these dimensions.

To use Apple's ecosystem as a familiar example, the iPad's introduction added a new *functional connection* and access point to the ecosystem. The development of iCloud added *integrated value* to almost all users of the Apple ecosystem. The iPhone 5s also represented a new functional connection, similar to the iPad. But certain iPhone 5s features, such as fingerprint recognition, added integrated value to the ecosystem, as well.

All of these additions to Apple's peerless ecosystem relied on technology and data considerations as the two essential factors in their development. Tending an ecosystem requires the analysis of user data to develop a deep understanding of how features within the ecosystem are being experienced. At the same time, it's important to track new and emerging technologies that might either enhance or threaten the ecosystem's health. Just like sunlight and water, technology and data are interdependent, working off each other in promoting growth. Together they are the two indispensable activities necessary for guiding all decisions in developing an ecosystem of value.

o Spotting Trends in Technology

Sometime around 2003, the landscape of consumer technologies was changing so rapidly that clients were coming to R/GA for advice on how to keep up. One major client in particular told us that they needed to lean on us to stay abreast of developments that were still not ready for market but were just coming up on the horizon. The client company's executives had serious concerns that they might get blindsided by a competitor using technologies they hadn't even been unaware of.

The truth was that we were dealing with our own problems in keeping up. At the time, R/GA had no formalized system in place for staying up-to-date with technology news, rumors, theory, and thought leadership. We subscribed to some technology trend-watching services, but we also knew that we had staff members for whom staying current with tech was a passion. Many of them were better informed than the research services we paid for. Back in 2003, when mobile technology was just about to break out into the era of the smartphone, we had in our offices a small informal working group that was obsessed with the possibilities created by mobile handheld computing.

So we asked these people, who were already engaged in daily conversations about the coming decade in tech, to help clue us in. We set up a system whereby anytime they saw something on a blog or a tech website that foretold a development way out on the bleeding edge of mobile communications, they would send a bookmark to a designated in-house editor. The outcome was *Futurevision*, a daily digest of tech news that is still distributed inside R/GA and among our clients.

In its earliest incarnation, *Futurevision* was printed in booklet form, but now it's a mostly online publication. *Futurevision* started by defining what we thought at the time were maybe six areas that were exploding with tech news of interest to our clients, including mobile communications, in-home entertainment, and digital out-of-home displays and kiosks.

Futurevision proved to be more than a simple clearinghouse for information. It became a focal point for debate and further exploration of the tech world. Articles prompted healthy but intense differences of opinion inside R/GA, which sometimes led us to invite outside experts to the office to help set us straight. We also used *Futurevision*'s format to organize our own presentations to clients, based on subjects applied to specific industries. For instance, we used all six *Futurevision* subject areas as the framework for an in-depth presentation on potential disruption in the banking industry.

Every company pursuing a functionally integrated ecosystem should be circulating something like *Futurevision*. Without such an internal clearinghouse of tech news and information, you're not likely to be getting the full benefit of your staff's knowledge. The fourth principle of Functional Integration, "reimagine value creation," requires everyone to have his or her imagination stoked regularly by new information, new developments, and new disruptive threats to your existing business models.

Back in 2003, we at R/GA were still getting used to the notion that mobile and online technologies would change everything we knew about our own business, as well as everything our clients knew about their respective businesses. In the years since then, it has become increasingly important to tap the knowledge and perspectives of that handful of passionate individuals inside every company who are obsessed with getting a read on what's coming down the road. The only thing worse than having a start-up threaten to take away a share of your business is to recognize the size of the threat too late to do anything about it.

For much of the 20th century, technologies were disruptive only in ways that were good for big companies. Technology has always been a positive force for efficiency and vertical integration. It has long played the dutiful role of back-office cost center by managing supply chains systems, databases, and customer files, always with the emphasis on cost effectiveness and streamlined operations. Even when the Internet first arrived, consumer-facing services in the form of e-commerce and company websites were rolled out in a similar spirit of efficiency.

For these reasons, managers in many larger companies might not recognize how, with the rise of Functional Integration, new consumer-facing services are inherently disruptive. New generations of technologies are being tested by countless start-ups in hopes of exploiting their full disruptive potential. It's safe to assume that there is more than one start-up working feverishly to undermine your most profitable product line or service with a disruptive offering. The question is whether you are ready to meet that eventuality with your own disruptive product.

○ Combining Technology

Speed to market, which has always been an important business consideration, has become an almost essential one today, and one that requires more than simply knowing the capabilities of new technologies. It requires continually experimenting with these technologies in combination with each other in order to create the best possible products and services.

R/GA conducts experiments of this kind in the Software Platform Lab, where we combine hundreds of different emerging technologies to allow the creative and technical staff to run fast simulations of new software code across multiple platforms, either in isolation or in combination. The lab is where technology mash-ups are born. Lab testing reveals which technologies are most suitable for enabling a new piece of software to deliver a satisfying digital experience to the end user. It also exposes potential "speeds and feeds" problems and other performance issues that might require further refinements.

The prime benefits of having a software platform lab are both speed and efficiency. The development cycle that runs from idea to software to testing to rethinking the original idea moves so fast that verdicts on next steps come quick. The ease of experimenting with combinations of technologies enables us to make efficient decisions earlier in the process prior to making irreversible decisions. By giving us a way of assessing software performance and brand experience on various platforms, we're able to make fast technology choices that benefit the user experience the most, which is always the ultimate goal.

If you lack the ability to test software combinations quickly and effectively, the technological barriers to innovation in your core areas can seem daunting. Some companies can rely on agencies such as R/GA for these services, but for companies engaging in Functional Integration, these capabilities are far too mission-critical to be farmed out. As the need for speed in software development intensifies, it becomes increasingly difficult to optimize functionally integrated devices and services without the help of an in-house software lab.

There may be personnel issues to deal with in moving such work inside, as the interdisciplinary collaborative style of software lab operations may prove to be a poor fit with the internal cultures of most IT departments. The software lab embodies the principles of an adaptive or agile process, which marks a significant departure from the more traditional waterfall process. With waterfall development, a lot of work goes into planning at the start, during which time you define the desired end product and create a baseline for performance that you subsequently track against. This is the kind of planning that IT offices normally undertake in order to install new computer hardware or implement a new software project.

Adaptive planning and development, in contrast, begins with the expectation that innovation will require plenty of change in the end product's definition all along the way. The rhythms of adaptive development are determined by repeated cycles of learn and change, learn and change. That is how every functionally integrated element is developed, through incremental building and iterative refining.

In the development of innovative products, adaptive planning pushes everyone on a given team to prepare workable software ready for stakeholder evaluation in two-week cycles, or sprints. Not all software engineers are comfortable working this way, because it breaks from the conventional practice of having software code spec'd out first and then written up according to those specs. Adaptive planning sprints are more productively organized in what we call a "sandbox." Redolent of the name, the sandbox consists of a figurative play area with a set of platforms in the software lab running versions of software in various iterative stages, allowing designers, engineers, and sometimes operational personnel all to contribute and "play" in the sandbox of the software's development.

Each sprint wraps up with the delivery of usable software to all stakeholders for testing at their desktops, laptops, and smartphones. That step enables decision makers to weigh in with comments and directions that will inform the work of the next sprint. At the finish line of every sprint, you will find the starting line of the next sprint.

The sprint process should not be confused with that down-to-the-wire rush to meet deadlines for marketing campaign launches or a new product introduction. Functionally integrated products and services engage in continuous sprint cycles. Constant iteration is their normal condition. One particular three-year project for an R/GA client has been delivered over the course of 59 end-to-end two-week and three-week sprints. The product team keeps iterating and trying new things in response to user data, technological change, and stakeholder comments and directives. Through one major hardware revision and frequent software updates, the product remains in a perpetual state of optimization and improvement.

o Prototyping Technology

It is one thing to read up on and debate technological change. It's quite another to hold the changes in your hand. Developing digital devices that users will wear or carry requires a process of prototype development similar to that of software development. At R/GA we believe that the best way to learn about a new technology is to try to solve a consumer need or desire within the constraints of that technology. Google Glass is a great example.

In 2013, when the number of Google Glass owners was highly restricted by its $2,000 price tag, we set out to use Google Glass as a solution for people with a specific need for hands-free navigation—urban cyclists. Our software designers wrote and street-tested code that streams wireless data and directions from New York's bike-sharing program platform into Google Glass. Test cyclists using Google Glass eyewear loaded with R/GA software were able to navigate the New York streets, read their locations, and tell how much time they had left on their rentals, all on the tiny Google Glass screen.

A Google Glass integration with any functionally integrated exercise service would allow runners and gym visitors to keep an eye on the time and the stages of their exercises without pausing to look at their smartphones or other devices. There are countless hurdles to be overcome before any such ideas reach wide public acceptance, but in an era marked by disruption, it is foolhardy not to explore the possibilities of Google Glass as a potential opportunity—or as a potential threat.

One way to think of such prototyping exercises is that they simulate the customer experience in ways that enable you to communicate conceptual ideas in more concrete terms. By explaining complex technical ideas through actual demonstrations, prototypes help inform and improve decision making about the feasibility and desirability of a concept. The most common misconception about prototyping is that it is fast and cheap work. Prototyping is a serious activity that should be considered an integral part of any digital service development process. It can be employed in design studies, technical feasibility tests, concept validation exercises, and user testing, just to name a few of its many applications.

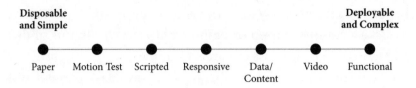

Figure 6.1 The Prototyping Continuum

As illustrated in Figure 6.1, the prototypes range in fidelity, from simple and disposable to complex and deployable. Your choices on this continuum will be based on the goals of the prototype, time available, and technical implications. For example, if the goal of the prototyping process is to prove that a technology works, then the focus will be on tech feasibility and not so much on design or user interaction.

Before you embark on any prototyping project, we recommend that you answer the following questions: What is the goal of the prototype? What customer/user need does it address? Who is the intended audience? What are the creative or technical parameters? It's also critical to think of prototyping as a series of experiments you will learn from. Every prototype we build is designed with feedback loops to ensure that we carry forward learning from a technical, design, and strategic perspective. We also say that the handoff of the prototype to the development team is as important as the prototyping process itself. If everything learned during the prototyping process has not been communicated to the production team, then the reason for a prototype's failure might be that the knowledge transfer has failed.

The advent of 3-D printing has been an invaluable aid in the creation of an R/GA prototyping lab, enabling us to play around with ideas for adding connective devices to our clients' ecosystems. The prototype lab also helps us prepare for the possibility that household penetration of 3-D printers will provide companies with opportunities for new functionally integrated services. In

2014, with fairly few household 3-D printers in circulation, we were discussing how some companies might someday want to provide their customers with do-it-yourself parts replacement software programs.

○ Accelerating Technology

When looking to the future of tech, every company needs to start taking that future into its own hands. As the leaders of some major carmakers have done, it's wise to recognize that if you don't conceive your company as a technology company, you are liable to be damaged or even bankrupted by one that does. As tech start-ups enter your industry unbidden with disruptive technologies in hand, looking at them with hostility is neither desirable nor even necessary. Through the use of what are called accelerator programs, established companies can obtain invaluable sneak peeks at some of the best new technological thinking in their respective industries, with the opportunity to invest in them. All it usually takes is a willingness to keep an open mind and to part with a relatively small amount of cash—the one thing start-ups never have enough of.

A group called Techstars now partners very selectively with what it calls "the top 1% of brands" in creating special accelerator programs matching start-ups with established companies. Start-ups compete for one of a dozen or so spots, allowing them to work for three months inside major companies and collaborate on what are frequently functionally integrated software and hardware projects. The start-ups are able to showcase their work and demonstrate their collaborative working styles in hopes of early-stage investment of up to $120,000 by the larger company.

In 2012, with the help of Techstars, Microsoft invited 11 start-ups onto its campus to work on projects related to Kinect, its motion-sensing input device. Although Kinect has been introduced as a game-playing enhancement that allows Microsoft's Xbox platform to compete with the Wii platform, Microsoft has been eager to develop an ecosystem around Kinect that involves more than just games. Accelerator start-ups developed Kinect applications for such varied uses as virtual reality medicine, physical and cognitive therapy, retail displays, and even "smart" fitting rooms for clothing stores.[3]

Other companies, including Sprint, Nike, and even R/GA, have also partnered with Techstars to launch accelerator programs. For companies eager to jump-start an ecosystem of value, there is perhaps no quicker way to trade complementary skills and know-how—and potentially spread one's bets on the future through somewhat modest venture capital investments. In R/GA's case, the accelerator program was used to identify and work with the 10 most exciting new start-ups in the area of the Internet of Things. The start-ups selected for the accelerator offered us a three-month look at their work and the opportunity for us to invest in them. In return they gained access to R/GA resources outside their areas of expertise, including integrated product design, service design, experience strategy, data strategy, branding, marketing, business modeling, and product engineering.

○ Focusing on the Right Data

Ecosystems are great at generating user data, but efforts to grow the ecosystem can be thwarted by misinterpretations of that data. In the weeks following the soft launch of an R/GA client's new digital service, we became aware that this particular client was repeatedly citing a goal of reaching 100,000 registered users. We believed that this benchmark was intended to determine whether the new service would pass a proof-of-concept milestone. If 100,000 people signed up for it, then it was ready for prime time. But the metric was actually derived from the horizontal integration playbook of media — capturing eyeballs. In our client's mind, registered users were a proxy for the number of unique visitors who would use the service and consequently visit the site on a monthly basis — to generate advertising revenue. Week by week, registrations rose, and as the goal drew near, the client grew happier, but for the wrong reasons.

The client and his team were also happy to note that users were spending almost 10 minutes on the site, a good number that in their minds suggested that the visitors were highly engaged in the site's offerings. But the clients stopped their analysis short. They decided not to probe any deeper to discover what had motivated users to visit the site in the first place. They also weren't curious enough to discover what the users found satisfying or dissatisfying about the site experience. Nor did they engage visitors after they left the site to learn why they weren't coming back. As we saw it, this client company completely missed an early opportunity to experiment with the audience and learn how it should adapt and improve its digital value proposition, because they were satisfied with media-based metrics rather than engagement and utility-based metrics.

The source of the problem, which we've seen many times before, is that horizontally integrated companies tend to cling to a familiar set of preferred key performance indicators (KPIs) that are not at all aligned with the goals of Functional Integration. For instance, the chief KPI for all e-commerce sites is the conversion rate from visitor to buyer. This makes sense for e-commerce. An e-commerce site with a low conversion rate is a site that needs work. But what doesn't make sense is applying similar horizontally integrated KPIs to measure the effectiveness of a functionally integrated service.

When it comes to digital services and experiences, the typical KPIs include the number of unique visitors to a new website, the number of app downloads, the number of times new content gets shared. There are two problems with these approaches to measurement. One is that they tend to treat digital products and services as they might hard goods (clothing) and physical services (pizza delivery). But digital products and services can be adapted and tweaked in response to data much more quickly and far less expensively than their counterparts in the physical realm. By missing this distinction, companies have learned to grow incurious about data that can provide the basis for digital improvement.

The second problem is that these kinds of metrics fail to offer any insights into the level of utility and benefit that users are obtaining from the ecosystem. Without such insights, there is no way to gauge the ecosystem's health or the extent to which it is accreting value. The main objective of KPI measurement in Functional Integration is to provide a guide for improving delivery of value. Companies should focus on those KPIs that will help them understand their users' deeper behaviors and motivations.

The chief KPIs of a functionally integrated ecosystem are usage and frequency of usage. Analyzing data for these two data points may seem obvious, but too often they are drowned out by other considerations, derived from horizontal integration. One hundred thousand registrations, for instance, does not necessarily signify that 100,000 people are actually using the tool. Nor does a 10-minute visit necessarily indicate engagement. It might just be that the tool is operating slowly or that it takes a long time to navigate.

Breaking down usage and frequency even further can help you determine actionable KPIs for digital services within an ecosystem. As illustrated in Table 6.1, there are three stages of usage and frequency that should be actively measured: acquisition, activation, and adoption. The first stage of acquisition is marked by passive usage, which is important because it represents

Table 6.1 Digital Service KPIs

	Usage (How Many and % Change)	Frequency (When and How Often)
Acquisition	Number of registrations or downloads Percentage change in registrations or downloads	Registrations or downloads per time period (hour, day)
Activation	Number of single-cycle events and percentage change: • Profiles completed • Features used • Content accessed • Tasks started vs. tasks completed	Occurrences of activities: • Time of day • Day of week Engagement of activities: • Number of times accessed in a given time period
Adoption	Number of repeat users and percentage change Popular features and activities used	Features and activities accessed most often Duration of usage for features and activities

the maximum number of people who have touched your service. It can be measured by metrics like number of registrations, number of app downloads, and number of purchases. In terms of frequency, you want to pay attention to when people are signing up and what's driving the timing of registrations. Are certain times of day, days of the week, or external factors like advertising and events driving acquisition?

The activation stage is marked by one cycle of usage, which is a valuable measure because it separates visitors who simply register and leave from those who actually begin using your service. It also provides insight into the activities and features that are popular. Activation can be measured by the number of people who complete a user profile and then use a tool, play a video, or engage in some other activity. The frequency of activation is also revealing, because it uncovers usage patterns related to the order, times of day, and days of the week during which certain features are used.

The final stage, adoption, is marked by repeat or ongoing usage. Adoption reveals the people who are ready to help you grow the ecosystem. They are finding enough utility from your service to keep using it. Measures in this stage are identical to those in the activation stage, except that the interpretation focus shifts to detecting which features the adopters are coming back to use and how often they are using certain features.

It's important to note that in today's overcrowded market for mobile apps, gaining adoption is no easy task. Marketing and social media strategies can generate awareness and numbers of trial users, but even the best apps are often used once and forgotten. Your product competes not only for value but also for behaviors. People who use your digital services need to be trained to remember the product's existence through repetitive triggers that can stimulate the behaviors that lead to habitual usage.

o Earning Your Data

The best way to learn from data is to actively engage and experiment with people who are using your digital services and interacting with digital touchpoints. Functionally integrated tools work best when they "earn" the user's data by offering value in exchange. What if a consumer willingly provides a brand with expressions of his or her hopes, goals, desires, achievements, failures, tastes, dislikes, and other explicit personal information? This kind of data allows a company to create optimization at the individual level (a maximum degree of personalization). It also provides the company with the ability to discern broader trends across the entire customer population, helping inform future decisions about the direction of the ecosystem and the business as a whole. The brand has earned the right to get this very explicit and actionable data from consumers because the consumer has willingly provided it to the brand, and they continue to provide the data on the basis of their ongoing interactions with the digital service.

This is exactly the kind of data that Amazon possesses about all its customers in what is probably the largest treasure trove of earned data on the planet. Nike possesses data about Nike+ runners that includes what their goals are, how often they run, how far, when and where. McCormick knows what flavors FlavorPrint users like and dislike, what recipes they prefer, which products they have purchased and have in the pantry — as well as ones they have yet to buy.

We use the term "earned data" as an analog to what is known as "earned media" in social networking and social media terms. Marketing and advertising professionals put a high premium on earned media, such as when a consumer "likes" a product on Facebook, shares a link to a YouTube video, or retweets a brand message. Earned media, which has also been called shared media, is both cheaper and more effective than paid media (advertising) or owned media (marketing through the brand's own websites). On average, Facebook users have about 130 friends. When a Facebook user likes or comments on a piece of brand content, that comment is potentially seen by an additional 130 people, which earns the brand exposure to audiences of consumers with no additional media expenditure.

Earned data enjoys the same status as earned media in that it is very personal and it is offered for free. It is a cornerstone of functionally integrated ecosystems, because it provides the basis for deepening the relationship between the customer and the brand. With Functional Integration, the more data the user shares with the brand, the more distinctive the service the brand is able to provide.

When most people talk about "big data" as it pertains to marketing, they are often talking about a paid form of data — data that can be bought from data providers. These providers include all of the various ad-serving vendors that enable brands to retarget consumers based on their online behaviors, or huge database vendors like Acxiom that have "data" about nearly every consumer in America.

These data sets are growing by the day, informed by tons of clickstream behavior that is appended to the sorts of demographic information that firms like Acxiom claim to have about individual consumers. All of this fits neatly into the space of paid data, and it's similar to paid media. A brand would need to buy this data from a data vendor in order to use it. All paid data is based on trying to discern intent from a mix of behavior and demographics. It's simply a guess about what each of us might want and what a brand might try to sell us. All paid data is implied; none of it is explicit.

Many brands also have a lot of owned data. They just don't use the data for Functional Integration purposes. The airlines have enjoyed owned data for years thanks to their loyalty programs. People are willing to allow airlines to aggregate data about them in exchange for the chance at free tickets in the future. Data of this kind fuels a lot of CRM-type programs, whether it's an airline or a credit card or a retailer with a loyalty program. Brands with e-commerce sites also aggregate owned data via consumer purchases online. This data might be a lot more accurate than the paid types of data, but it's also somewhat implied. The frequency with which you fly on a particular airline does not necessarily imply or predict where you will go on vacation this summer.

Data is a cornerstone to functionally integrated ecosystems, in which assessment of earned data yields earned intelligence. Functional Integration enables companies to access new sources of data about their customers thanks to principle one: utility is relevance. Functionally integrated digital services hinge on utility, providing value to consumers. Consumers, in turn, pour tons of personal data into these digital services.

Companies and brands that use earned data will be at a distinct competitive advantage over the ones reliant on paid data and even owned data. In fact, this might spell doom for the horizontal integrators that fail to make the leap, as the functionally integrated companies will make smarter business decisions based on the data, as well as provide services and offers to customers at an individual, intimate level. They become more personalized, more relevant, more empathetic, and more oriented to addressing the true needs of their customers.

o Navigating the Road Map of Functional Integration

Armed by your ability to monitor, react to, and leverage new sources of data and technology capabilities, you will be better prepared to guide the evolution of a functionally integrated ecosystem. Specifically, there are two critical dimensions of decision making—the dimension of adding value to the ecosystem and the dimension of connecting the ecosystem (see Figure 6.2). You will need to make decisions about how and when to improve, remove, or expand functionality of products and services within the ecosystem. You will also need to make decisions about how and when to integrate certain components of the ecosystem or to open the ecosystem up to the rest of the world.

Adding Functional Value

Analyzing earned data ultimately makes products better and more relevant to customers, which draws them closer into the ecosystem, which in turn accretes value within the ecosystem. The functionally integrated relationship with customers, built on earned data, tends to feed a virtuous cycle of innovation in well-managed ecosystems. The Nike ecosystem's evolution through the Nike+ platform serves as vivid case history of how both functional value and integrated value have been added to the ecosystem over time, through the careful interpretation of

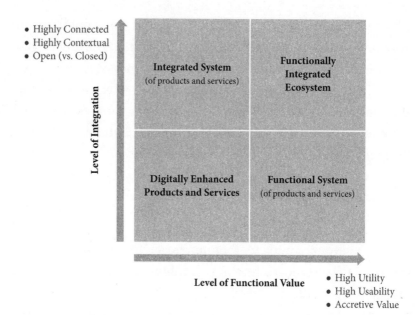

- Highly Connected
- Highly Contextual
- Open (vs. Closed)

Level of Integration

Integrated System
(of products and services)

Functionally
Integrated
Ecosystem

Digitally Enhanced
Products and Services

Functional System
(of products and services)

Level of Functional Value

- High Utility
- High Usability
- Accretive Value

Figure 6.2   Navigating the Road to Functional Integration Along Two Dimensions

earned data and the accommodation and application of emerging technologies. At every decision point, when advancing technology offered up new threats and opportunities, insights drawn from earned data helped guide the way toward new products and services that have both deepened and broadened the appeal of the Nike ecosystem.

The founding of the Nike+ platform, described in Chapter Three, was based on a partnership with Apple iTunes, one that married music with running. Offering integrated functionality in five ways, the original Nike+ iPod

1. Enabled runners to set goals for themselves
2. Integrated personal music into the running experience through the iPod

3. Provided informative voice prompts during the run to let runners know how fast they were moving, how far they'd gone, and how much farther they needed to go
4. Provided a seamless data transfer and storage process that automatically happened every time a runner synced his or her iPod—meaning runners didn't have to adopt a new behavior
5. Enabled runners to track and save progress of all their runs on the Nike+ website, delivered in an attractive visualized format

Because of the close integration of the iPod with Nike's running data, the partner companies saw plenty of opportunities to deepen the running experience by marketing iTunes music as a running companion. All sorts of music-related features were made available for purchase through Apple's iTunes store, including favorite playlists of famous athletes and custom playlists of songs particularly well suited to the rhythms of running. When the initial user reaction to these features wasn't as strong as anticipated, the graphic design on the Nike+ website was tweaked to make the offerings a little more prominent.

No matter. What Nike+ members pored over most on the Nike+ site was their own running data. The product had been conceived as a marriage of music and running, with music being the big attraction. But most users embraced it the other way around. Nothing interested the runners more than the information Nike+ provided them about themselves.

Nike officials were hardly surprised. They understood the appeal of running data, or they wouldn't have developed Nike+ in the first place. What they hadn't expected, what they needed the data to tell them, was the depth of interest in running data to the exclusion of other features. As the Nike+ community has grown to more than 21 million and the terabytes of earned data have piled up, Nike has come to know its customers better than any other sportswear maker in the world.

Although the iTunes offerings had some fans, over a period of time the runner playlists were dropped from the Nike+ website. A feature called Tag, which was a virtual game that allowed runners to compete with each other, shared a similar fate some years later. Usage wasn't high enough to warrant keeping it around, so Tag was removed in subsequent software updates. Such decisions reflect the fact that you actually add value to an ecosystem by subtracting low-performing features that produce clutter. Although there is little financial cost to carrying a feature with few followers, it's better to remove the feature and replace it with something else. The key is to set aside fears of upsetting a few vocal fans. Clutter exacts a cost in user experience from all members, and the importance of protecting user experience cannot be stressed enough.

Ecosystems of all kinds, including natural ones, are weakened when they fail to flush out waste. The best functionally integrated companies tend to pare back underperforming features in the ecosystem in order to avoid cluttered user experiences. In 2012, Apple unplugged Ping, its two-year-old music-based social network.[4] Google has become infamous for killing off features in its ecosystem if they fail to prove their stickiness with users. Google's so-called spring cleanings in 2011 and 2013 brought doom to 70 digital products and services, including Google Reader, which inspired outcry from its small but loyal following.[5] Google's rationale, informed by earned data, is that there is no point in devoting resources to services that fail to show evidence of growth. Oftentimes, there is nothing specifically wrong with an unpopular feature. It's just that, as with Ping, other services were already satisfying that particular user need.

A general principle of Functional Integration is that the relevance of data is measured by its propensity to inform and change behavior. Nike+ devices create value by helping you set goals for running and telling you how well you've met them. There are several direct competitors to Nike+ wearable devices, including FitBit and Jawbone, but Nike's ecosystem enjoys two areas of competitive advantage in the face of such competition. First, Nike+ hosts the largest athletic brand community of runners in the world. The Runkeeper app has more runners on it. Second, Nike has its enviable troves of earned data.

Leveraging the first asset, the Nike+ community, was fairly easy through marketing and public events such as the worldwide Human Race. But the second asset, earned data, had been largely untapped at Nike prior to 2011. Then a new insight emerged within the company, that with the growth in the so-called Quantified Self movement and with so many competing wristbands tracking miles, calories, and heart rates, to define the metric is to define the market.

The challenge Nike took on was to create a new, proprietary metric, but *one that offered users special value.* The last point was key, in keeping with Functional Integration's business model, which includes the trading of data for value. Nike didn't want to create a new proprietary metric of activity to put up an artificial wall between Nike and the rest of the athletic world. Rather, they wanted to offer the world a metric of activity that would offer new value to people.

As it is, all other wristband activity trackers share a specific weakness in their mode of measurement. They use tiny accelerometers to calculate calories burned according to activity levels. But accurate measurement is impossible without first calculating the wearer's weight. If a 200-pound man and his 130-pound wife go for a run together, the 200-pound man will always burn more calories because he's carrying 200 pounds. And what about people who don't go for runs? How might that activity be calculated in order to provide *relevance* to the health benefits of everyday activity? If you took a wearable device to work and it measured your activity throughout the day, perhaps you'd take the stairs or walk to lunch in order to increase your score.

The result of these insights was the development of the Nike+ FuelBand and its accompanying proprietary data algorithm, the NikeFuel point, a unit of activity measurement that affords nonrunners a way to participate in the Nike+ community. The proprietary measurement of all daily activity on a wearable device provides relevance to users because it motivates and documents positive changes in behavior. It represents a bid to grow the value of the Nike ecosystem by broadening its appeal, thanks to Nike's mountain of earned data (Figure 6.3).

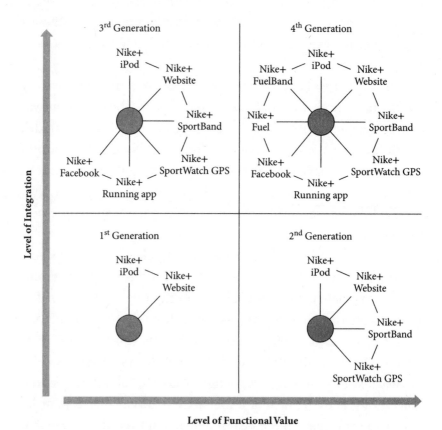

Figure 6.3   How Nike Added Functional Value to Its Ecosystem

Adding Integrated Connections

Nike's expansion of the functional value within its ecosystem has been matched only by its systematic extension of integrated connections to that ecosystem. Each new integrated connection offers a new portal into the ecosystem for a different consumer segment. Then, each new user, by joining the ecosystem, strengthens it by contributing his or her data. Proper interpretation of this data is critical to the success of every ecosystem. Managers of well-run ecosystems study the user data earned from members to inform their decisions about the next round of functional innovations and integrated connections.

Nike's steady path down this road demonstrates how the interplay of technology and earned data played a determinative role at every stage of the trip. Around the time that Nike was looking to the 2008 Olympics in China as an opportunity to spread Nike+ to the world's largest market, they were armed with the knowledge that music wasn't a truly integral part of the Nike+ experience. Since the penetration of iPods was very low in China, selling Nike+ iPod there didn't seem like the right solution. Instead, the Beijing summer Olympics gave Nike a target date to produce the Nike+ SportBand as a second integrated connection to the Nike ecosystem. The SportBand was designed as an alternative to Nike+ iPod, featuring all the functions that previously were carried by the receiver attached to the iPod, contained inside an affordable yet innovative sport watch. It signified a new entry point to Nike+ for runners who didn't want to listen to music, didn't want to carry an iPod, or, as was the case for many runners, didn't care to buy an iPod.

The proliferation of iPhones with GPS tracking created another opportunity for Nike to expand the Nike+ ecosystem in 2010. Simple and cheap iPhone running apps such as Runkeeper were competing with Nike+ iPod and the Nike+ SportBand,

and Nike wasted no time in launching its own low-cost app. The decision had some significant implications for the Nike ecosystem. For starters, now runners could use any brand of sneaker to join the Nike+ community, because they didn't need Nike shoes with the special tiny well in the sole to hold a transmitter. Second, the app would enable Nike runners to track their runs for one-tenth the price of the iPod Sport Kit. However, Nike had already learned from Nike+ feedback that runners wanted better route tracking, which was only available via the iPhone's GPS feature. So Nike made the calculation that providing yet another entry point into the ecosystem, with incremental functional value, was worth the loss of SportBand and Nike+ iPod revenue.

The FuelBand not only provided a new connection to Nike+ for a demographic that might never have bought Nike products before but also provided Nike with the opportunity to open up the Nike+ platform for the first time through an application programming interface (API). Scaling the ecosystem with an open API is often the only way to generate geometric growth in ecosystem members because open systems touch many more people on any given day and provide them with the opportunity to join, an opportunity that they otherwise never would have had if the system had remained closed. Many of the features passed over for the first FuelBand release, such as adding sleep tracking and rewards for run-related charitable giving, have been picked up by other digital services, extending Nike's reach into other communities at almost no cost.

In 2010 when Nike launched the Nike+ app, the new app included seamless integration with Facebook to expand social interaction beyond the Nike+ running community into a runner's broader circle of friends and family. The app also gamified the running experience through badges and performance levels, encouraging runners to push themselves and share their achievements with others.

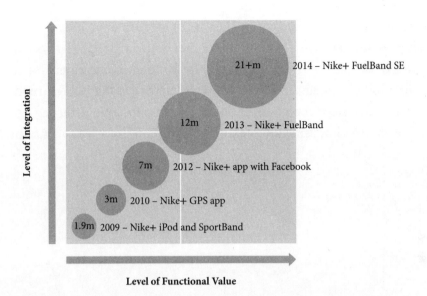

Figure 6.4 The Nike+ Community Expanded with the Ecosystem

Each of these decisions to scale served to accelerate the size of the Nike+ community. Prior to the GPS-enabled app, Nike+ membership hovered around 1.9 million. A year afterward, it expanded to over 3 million. Then after Nike launched the Running app with Facebook social integration, user numbers ballooned to over 7 million (see Figure 6.4).

o   o   o

The histories of the Amazon, Apple, and Google ecosystems all show similar patterns in the iterative interplay between earned data and technology advancement. Without one or the other, Functional Integration is impossible. Jeff Bezos's comment that the Kindle is a digital service that only looks like a device could also apply to the Apple iPad or Google Glass. The function of each device is to draw you into its maker's ecosystem of digital services, where you'll make purchases and contribute your user data, helping make the ecosystem just a little more appealing to the next potential user. That kind of merger of the digital and physical worlds is only possible through the proper management of a functionally integrated ecosystem, by allowing the data earned from ecosystem members to inform each subsequent foray into new devices and integrated connections.

7

Cultivating an Ecosystem of Value

Principle Seven: Lead like the world depends on it.

In late 2005, Nokia was preparing the release of its N-series of phones, which at the time were by far the world's most advanced smartphones in development. The N-series included the first smartphones ever to bring together such functions as GPS, Bluetooth, accelerometers, Wi-Fi, mobile Internet, and forward-facing cameras for video calls. Some models, designed especially for making videos, were outfitted with high-quality Carl Zeiss lenses.

Nokia touted the N-series as something much more than a phone. The company called it a "multimedia computer."[1] N-series models were shipped with built-in converters for viewing files saved in PDF, Word, Excel, and PowerPoint. They also had lots of fun software for games and moviemaking. The N-series ad slogan, translated into many languages, was "It's what computers have become."[2]

R/GA was chosen by Nokia's marketing department to help with the launch of the N-series, set for 2006. (The iPhone, just a rumor at the time, would not come out until June 2007.) We had proposed that the best way to market phones with such advanced capabilities was to build web-linked services that would be unique to the N-series. The idea was that instead of just telling the public how cool the new phones are, Nokia should give its customers special tools to experience that coolness in their own lives. The leaders of Nokia's marketing division liked the idea, and they funded R/GA and a few other partners to build it out.

The result was a service called viNe—with the "N" capitalized to highlight both Nokia and the N-series. The viNe software linked to the phone's GPS receiver and enabled customers to upload pictures and video to their personalized viNe webpages while on the go. With viNe you had an automated, intuitive system that allowed you to share where you'd been and what you'd seen, in real time. In a sense, viNe functioned as a mobile multimedia social networking software program, although no one called it that at the time.

Nokia's software architecture made the task of writing and distributing viNe exceptionally easy, as the Symbian operating system was an open system. Anyone could write Symbian software and make it available for download to Nokia phones. We designed viNe to work best on model N-95, the flagship of the N-series, and it really managed to showcase all of that device's advanced technology. viNe was a killer app that gave prospective customers a compelling, concrete reason for choosing Nokia's best, most profitable phone. What could be wrong with that?

It turned out that Nokia's systems division, which oversaw Nokia-authorized mobile applications, already had something similar in the works that would be much bigger and better than viNe. Why should one Nokia division start signing up customers to a fairly modest digital service now, when another Nokia division was preparing a superior service that would eventually supersede it?

The obvious answer is that as soon as the systems division was ready with its big new thing, it would be very easy to shift all the viNe registrations over. Instead, after a succession of internal discussions, Nokia's marketing division settled the turf battle quietly by deferring to the systems division. Although viNe was years ahead of its time, and although the systems division never did come up with anything like it, Nokia let viNe die on the vine.

○ The Leadership Factor

We tell the story of viNe as a cautionary tale. Nokia was the world leader in mobile phones at the time. It had a lot of gifted, talented people who were great to work with. The Nokia marketing division was forward thinking enough to embrace viNe as a marketing tool. But in this instance, Nokia's consensus-oriented leadership culture permitted certain rigid organizational prerogatives to kill off an attractive service that was helping support one of the most important product launches in company history. Nokia's leaders deprived their customers of something fun, useful, and well regarded, in the name of smoothing some ruffled feathers in the systems division.

The moral of the story is that the inevitable final hurdle for success with Functional Integration is leadership. You can get the strategy right (Chapter Four), get the execution right (Chapter Five), and spend countless hours improving and refining the ecosystem (Chapter Six). But it all might come to nothing if corporate leadership doesn't appreciate that Functional Integration, like all business transformation, is bound to face resistance within the organization. Digital products and services represent a strategic response to disruption in the marketplace, so they naturally require some degree of disruption in the workplace as well. It's neither possible nor desirable to find neat and tidy compartments in the organization chart when starting something as fluid and organic as an ecosystem of value. Turf gets impinged on, toes get stepped on, feelings get hurt—and team capabilities get stretched and grow stronger as a result.

Less than a decade after viNe's uprooting, Nokia lost its position as the leader of the mobile phone industry. Nokia's global market share of smartphone sales tumbled from 40 percent in 2010 to less than 5 percent in 2012.[3] On November 19, 2013, Nokia shareholders voted to sell the company's entire consumer mobile phone division to Microsoft for $7.3 billion.[4]

It seems to us that viNe's demise was a symptom of what made Nokia's leadership culture incompatible with long-term success in the smartphone category. Nokia designed, engineered, and marketed its smartphones as stand-alone products without ever developing a functionally integrated ecosystem to support them. Rivals Palm, Motorola, Sony Ericsson, and BlackBerry's Research in Motion did the same. Prior to Apple's introduction of the iPhone in 2007, these five companies had the smartphone market virtually all to themselves. Then, over the next six years, all five had been forced out of the consumer smartphone market. Apple and Google, which had brought out the Android smartphone operating system in 2008, were two functionally integrated companies that swooped in and cleared out nearly all the horizontally integrated companies from the industry.[5]

The smartphone is the essential hub device for most of today's Functional Integration, so it shouldn't be surprising that the smartphone was the first consumer category to be dominated entirely by the two companies with the largest functionally integrated ecosystems in the world. The reason that leaders at Nokia, Palm, and the other failed smartphone makers could not adapt to this new reality is the same reason that the leaders of so many companies continue to bank on horizontal integration in the face of digital disruption and commoditization.

For corporate leaders selling directly to consumers, most know little else besides the making and marketing of products through mass media. The management ranks of their companies are also filled with people whose careers are built on the same horizontally integrated orientation. Digital disruption naturally appears to most of them not as a set of opportunities but as an alien threat. By continuing to do the things they know best, they may claim to be sticking to their knitting, so to speak, but what they are really doing is whistling past the graveyard.

From certain points of view within any organization, there is never a good time to engage disruptive innovation. Jeff Bezos has led Amazon from nothing to one of the largest retailers on earth, and even inside his own forward-looking organization, there are those who question whether bold moves into new categories constitute "distractions." Bezos told *Harvard Business Review* that such questions "all have at their heart one of the reasons that it's so difficult for incumbent companies to pursue new initiatives. It's because even if they are wild successes, they have no meaningful impact on the company's economics for years." Bezos compares the process of growing the Amazon ecosystem to "planting seeds." He acknowledges that it usually takes five to seven years before an individual seed ever develops into something with a meaningful impact on the company's revenues.[6]

That's the kind of patient, farsighted leadership required for sustained success in Functional Integration. The Nike+ iPod kit was predated by more than a decade of smaller product experiments at Nike. Progressive Insurance invested a dozen years or more in making its Snapshot service a viable revenue-producing feature in what is developing into an ecosystem of digital products and services. Licensing the patents yielded by all those years of innovation might well produce new streams of revenue that can set Progressive apart in the increasingly commoditized field of auto insurance. But in the seventh or eighth year of trying and failing with Snapshot prototypes, it's unlikely that such an outcome was foreseeable. Progressive's leadership persisted with Snapshot nonetheless.

All of the revenue-producing business models at your company today were once risky innovations that long ago had many of their unknowns and uncertainties sifted out through trial and error. Functional Integration requires embracing new unknowns and uncertainties, undertaking new trials and making new errors. Some people within the organization will be very uncomfortable with this prospect, which is yet another important reason why Functional Integration offers the potential for building a strong competitive advantage. If Functional Integration were easy, everyone would be doing it. Other companies in your industry also fear the unknown. If you choose to take the leap, others will likely take a while to follow.

Some companies are born with business transformation in their DNA. Others have transformation thrust on them, as their lone alternative to irrelevance or extinction. Both types of companies are places where leadership has a comparatively easier time accommodating Functional Integration. Both are likely to grasp the urgency of digital disruption, if for entirely different reasons.

Most companies, however, fall into a third category. They are neither transformative by nature nor in such desperate straits that transformation is their sole way forward. At such companies, leaders may hope to achieve transformation among many other objectives and goals. These are the companies most at risk of failing like Nokia.

With so many existing product lines to protect and so much success to defend, leaders at these companies will always be tempted to view Functional Integration strategies as potential distractions, with too many unattractive risks and drawbacks to deal with during *this* quarter or *this* fiscal year. The worst enemy of such companies is not a lack of ideas or a lack of vision. It is a lack of leadership to inspire corporate culture to engage with a set of limited and calculated but urgent risks. It is a lack of courage to plant the seeds that Jeff Bezos speaks of, seeds that might not grow and bear fruit for another five years or more.

Every transformative process encounters some natural degree of resistance from within. The specific challenges of leadership in executing a Functional Integration strategy come down to three main areas of focus: engaging the company's incumbent cultural issues, restructuring the organization to encourage the ecosystem's growth, and committing the ecosystem to an open and sustainable future. Leaders must first recognize the so-called incumbency issues for what they are, and get out ahead of them sooner than later. Then as the ecosystem of value begins to grow, it takes leadership to find a home and a budget for it, so that the ecosystem's development is not always in danger of being subordinated in priority to other activities.

Finally, it takes leadership to realize the full benefits of keeping the ecosystem platform open, growing, and contributing to a better world. The goal should be toward creating value not only for your customers but for all the digital developers and other companies that want to contribute to the ecosystem. As an antidote to horizontal integration, Functional Integration provides a cure for that system's inherent wastefulness of natural resources. Sustaining an ecosystem of value is perfectly aligned with sustaining the ecosystem that is planet Earth. In the coming years, it will be incumbent on you and your company to excel at sustaining both.

○ Lifting the Burden of Internal Obstacles

As a business model innovation, Functional Integration faces many of the same internal obstacles to success within the workplace that confront all innovation. In *Seizing the White Space*, Mark W. Johnson estimates that there are at least 19 common organizational measures that tend to thwart business model innovation in particular, including such considerations as unit pricing, time to break even, channel options, and throughput.[7]

All these measures are accompanied by common rules of thumb that have developed over time in order to contain risk in day-to-day operations. Developing an ecosystem of value, however, is nothing less than a frank launch into the unknown. Functional Integration is disruptive by design, because it requires new, unproven ways of doing things within organizations structured to avoid disruption in the name of efficiency and order. It always requires taking on some added risk, and because every company employs people whose jobs are to reduce exposure to risk, some resistance to building a functionally integrated ecosystem is inevitable.

There are at least five common issues that tend to thwart progress toward Functional Integration within a company: failure to grasp the importance of accreted value, reluctance to cannibalize existing products and services, mission creep from other initiatives, unrealistic expectations, and inadequate prioritization:

1. **Failure to grasp the importance of accreted value** has sometimes been an issue for companies accustomed to identifying media partners to help them control the costs of marketing campaigns. When developing that first new functionally integrated element, a client company might suggest sharing ownership of the service with partners in order to save some money leading up to launch. But the profit formula for

Functional Integration is all about capturing accreted value over time. The best ecosystems result from years of growth in the numbers and participation rates of registered members. Sharing access to those members by sharing ownership runs completely counter to the principle of accreted value.

Apple's ecosystem wouldn't be worth what it is today if Apple had chosen to partner with the recording companies and share user data about iTunes store transactions. The same goes for Amazon and its practice of not sharing customer data with book publishers. The accreted value of Apple's iTunes and app stores proceeds from the 575 million active credit card accounts that the App Store had on file as of June 2013, more than any other store on the Internet.[8] The size of that enormous customer base has led to rumors that Apple is eager to expand into the category of electronic payments. Google, with hundreds of millions of Gmail subscribers, has already made such a move with Google Wallet.

2. **Reluctance to cannibalize existing products** is one of the chief reasons Microsoft has never created a viable ecosystem to compete with Apple or Google. Microsoft has been loath to make moves that might cannibalize the PC market on which its quarterly profits from Windows rely. It has put out a succession of costly product failures such as Zune and Surface in halfhearted attempts to compete with Apple's iPod and iPad. Surface is in some ways a superior product to the iPad, but without being a part of a strong ecosystem of value, its sales failed to catch fire upon its introduction in 2012.[9]

Apple, in contrast, has a culture that does not fear cannibalization of its current product line. In January 2013, Apple CEO Tim Cook took some pride in telling investors that strong iPad sales had probably led to reduced sales of desktop and laptop Macs, just as iPhones had cut into iPod sales years earlier. "I see cannibalization as a huge opportunity for us," he said. "Our base philosophy is to never fear cannibalization. If we do, somebody else will just cannibalize it, and so we never fear it. We know that iPad will cannibalize some Macs, but that doesn't worry us."[10] The two companies starkly illustrate the difference between a company that has fully embraced Functional Integration and one that cannot.

3. **Mission creep from existing initiatives** often takes place when companies try to transfer many of their main capabilities into what they misperceive as a new communications medium. Digital services can be difficult to design, whereas content always appears to be a convenient substitute. Content clutter is a common result, as is feature clutter, whether or not those capabilities could make a positive contribution to the aims of the project.

   When R/GA worked with a publishing house that wanted to make its textbooks available in digital form online to college professors using the texts in their class syllabuses, the project became so bloated with features that development became bogged down in delays, followed by budget troubles. It would have been much faster to launch a basic product that offered professors their chief benefit, which was to make it easier to assemble chapters from various books as reading assignments. Under that course of action, additional features could have come out with future iterations of the software. Instead, when a new management team took over at the publishing house, the entire project was killed and never saw the light of day.

   A project facing delays from that kind of mission creep always risks sinking under its own weight. Digital services cannot be designed in ways that aim to satisfy someone's ideal of a perfect product. In the textbook publisher's case, no one had the power to define what constituted a minimally viable product suitable for release on schedule. As a result, the publishing house wasted its money and risked falling years behind its competitors in digitizing its content.

4. **Unrealistic expectations** are sometimes raised by clients who want us to assure them that the project we're helping them with will actually achieve certain sales, numbers of users, or other metrics. Although the question is not unreasonable, the expectation of an answer is unrealistic. Marketers are often asked to make such predictions in the world of horizontal integration. The answers come from market research, as there are tried-and-true methods for taking measure of your competitors and then putting out products that offer a desirable alternative to what those competitors are selling.

But Functional Integration is a game that involves winning by accretion in the long run, not by grabbing new market share in the short run. Although we have plenty of evidence about what it takes to succeed at it, as a business model it remains an innovative process that can't produce the predictive metrics many clients are accustomed to.

Unrealistic expectations for certainty in these cases tend to be shaped by management comfort with horizontal integration and its reliance on mass media advertising inside clear product categories. Everyone claims to like innovation, but there are those who are too risk averse to truly enjoy working with the unknown.

5. **Low prioritization** by leadership can allow Functional Integration initiatives to waste away from underfunding and understaffing. Unfamiliar products and services tend not to get the benefit of the doubt that innovation requires. In short, all attempts at innovation risk being orphaned by leaders who prefer not to be associated with the setbacks and short-term disappointments that innovation often brings.

Neglect of this kind can take many forms. The death of Nokia viNe, for instance, was due to a kind of upper-level lack of prioritization. In order to survive, viNe needed explicit support from the top. At the very least, the marketing division needed support in principle for its need to carry out its duties as it saw fit. Instead, leadership's priority was the achievement of a consensus between the two divisions. Because innovation by its very nature is new and untested, consensus-oriented decisions rarely leave any room for it.

o   o   o

Functional Integration projects are always in danger of falling victim to one or another of these kinds of internal issues, which are lying in wait inside any organization where leadership lacks the resolve to rein them in. In truth, these issues are all symptoms of the same disease. If leadership is not willing to get behind Functional Integration in the face of disruption, uncertainty, and risk, then functionally integrated innovations are bound to fail.

o Making Room for Functional Integration

Companies with a true ongoing commitment to Functional Integration must find ways to organize their personnel so that they are not lost and rendered ineffective by the influence of larger horizontally integrated operations. Functional Integration typically grows outward from one of three organizational functions: marketing, information systems, or R&D. There are a variety of reasons why each of these areas can be problematic as a long-term home to Functional Integration when it comes to incubating vital and growing ecosystems of value.

Leaving Functional Integration efforts to the marketing department is a common choice, because chief marketing officers are likely to see Functional Integration as an appropriate evolution of their area's activities. The chief problem is that CMO budgets are typically dedicated downward to brand managers who are accountable for the performance of their respective product lines. CMOs might have R&D budgets, but those dollars are ordinarily spent scrutinizing the efficiency of their spending on mass media advertising. There is rarely money to spare on Functional Integration projects that fail to show immediate return on investment.

The other likely location in the organization chart is information technology. The chief information officer can be counted on to understand or least be conversant in many of the technical demands of building a Functional Integration effort. A secondary benefit of locating Functional Integration with the CIO is that information systems don't face the same revenue-producing expectations that marketing does. A potential downside is that IT staff do not always work well with consumer-facing technologies. Housing the ecosystem in R&D poses a similar problem. All these departments have valuable contributions to make in building an ecosystem, but it's hard to pick one or another as an ideal fit.

Some positive results in Functional Integration have been generated through the "skunkworks" model, in which a work group is set apart from the rest of the company and tasked with developing the organization's Functional Integration initiatives. This is the model best used in the rare case of a client who for a variety of reasons might need to launch a fairly complete ecosystem of digital services all at once. Such a project is too complex to be executed as a side activity under marketing or information technology. Although the heads of those departments would be involved in the skunkworks process, the head of the skunkworks should report directly to the CEO.

The history of skunkworks points to its effectiveness as a model for collaborative innovation in a short timeline. The original Skunk Works was the name of the Lockheed aircraft company's secret airplane production facility during World War II, where the staff was charged with creating a high-speed fighter plane that could compete with the German Messerschmidt fighters. The same facility later produced the infamous U2 spy plane.[11]

IBM used the skunkworks model to develop the first IBM PC, and Motorola used it to develop the hot-selling Razr phone in the 2000s. In both cases, upper management hoped that by setting up small teams away from the main corporate headquarters, the teams would be sheltered from the constraints of everyday management responsibilities. Unlike R&D labs, however, skunkworks are expected to develop products that will be cost effective to manufacture and have appeal to the consumer. It's an organizational model that seems ideally suited to Functional Integration.

Funding Functional Integration in its early stages is another problem, one that can involve a variety of investment approaches. One fairly simple strategy is to break off a piece of the R&D budget expressly for innovative projects that do not conform to one brand or product line. That's what Procter & Gamble's Corporate Innovation Fund does. The fund functions like a venture capital seed fund, allocating approximately $75 million out of P&G's massive $2 billion R&D budget to projects that don't involve existing P&G brands.

The fund addresses a problem inside P&G's culture, where ideas that aren't forecast as blockbusters tend to get killed off without a second look. That's the same type of problem Functional Integration services and other disruptive ideas face in their early stages. It's not always obvious how they can be a source of any revenue, so they often face rapid judgment and dismissal before they can get funded and more fully explored.

Another way to create more funding opportunities for Functional Integration is through corporate venture capital programs, in which companies invest in outside efforts to develop projects that complement their goals. Harvard Business School professor

Josh Lerner has recognized that such funds have certain unique strengths. He says that "if you combine the scale and resources of the corporate lab with some of the intensity and urgency associated with the venture capital model, you have something that can be very, very strong."[12] BMW i Ventures is one such fund. Based in New York, the fund invests in "urban mobility services," which include car-sharing, location-based services, and parking technologies. These ventures are hardly at the top of today's BMW owner's concerns, but as we noted in Chapter Two, BMW is looking to a future in which the company might become a functionally integrated "mobility company," rather than just a horizontally integrated carmaker.

The Boston Consulting Group's 2012 study on corporate venture capital reported that more than 750 corporations around the world have such units in operation. According to BCG, "Venture investing appears well on its way to establishing a firm foothold in the corporate world as companies look to nascent companies not just to generate financial returns but also to complement their R&D efforts, penetrate fast-growing emerging markets, and gain early access to potentially disruptive technologies and business models."[13]

One relative newcomer to the venture scene, Google Ventures, rapidly became the top investor in venture-backed companies in the third quarter of 2012.[14] When Google bought Nest Labs in early 2014 for $3.2 billion, it marked the fourth time that a Google Ventures–funded company had been acquired by the corporate parent. At the time of the Nest Labs purchase, by one estimate, Google Ventures was completing two to three new investments every week.[15]

A corporate venture program normally uses a closed-end fund model that mirrors the targets and methods of independent venture capital firms. But at the same time, the program is a subsidiary inside the corporation. This means that the VC team must adhere to annual budgets, strategic business plans, and corporate governance, processes, and procedures. These constraints can enhance the fund's function, keeping it accountable — they don't have to get in its way. And by observing the successes of the venture group, executives might be encouraged to take bolder positions. The natural friction between the earnings-based corporate culture and the risk-based VC culture can enrich both.

Ethan Mollick, a professor of management science at the Wharton School, observes that companies are making more numerous bets. These bets are smaller and more spread out than ever, which Mollick regards as a kind of democratization of the innovation process. "One of the ways we get more innovation is by taking more draws," he says.[16] The result has been a rapid and radical change in how entrepreneurial innovation is funded.

What happens, though, when the ecosystem outgrows its start-up status? There aren't many precedents for this eventuality. Amazon, Apple, and Google are all fully functionally integrated companies. They serve as great models of how ecosystems develop and provide strong examples of the opportunities that ecosystems create, but they don't offer much practical guidance in how to nurture functionally integrated seedlings in the soil of horizontally integrated companies.

Nike provides the singular organizational exception. The Nike+ system first emerged as an initiative of Nike's marketing department. But in 2010, a group of Nike executives, including Stefan Olander, who had been an internal champion of Nike+ from the start, approached Nike CEO Mark Parker with a formal pitch for a Digital Sport division within the company. The concept was that Digital Sport would be a cross-category division that could develop the basic idea of Nike+ in other sports besides running.

Looking at the Nike example, we can see how any horizontally integrated company might take on a three-year organizational initiative toward digital transformation. Year one begins with uniting and functionally integrating the company's current digital offerings. In most companies, operating units such as sales, service, and marketing all have their own consumer-facing web offerings, and none of them are linked in ways that would optimize the company's ability to create, deliver, and capture value. Applying the seven principles of Functional Integration would result in the creation of a single digital customer portal that would put user utility first and begin to engage the advantages of multiple contexts and synergy that a true ecosystem would provide.

Leading into year two of digital transformation, the company would need to extend the organization of its digital resources into such areas as IT, R&D, and product design, united by a project management office that would lift some of the burdens of tracking such cross-functional digital operations. In the second year, it would also be valuable to open up a separate unit, a digital "center of excellence," a laboratory that could experiment with cutting-edge technologies, study competing digital products, and remain outside the daily work of the company.

True transformation takes place in the third year when the company is able to set up a separate unit for digital design and strategy, charged with the job of developing and cultivating the company's ecosystem of value. In the C-suite, such a division would fall under the purview of a CXO, a chief customer experience officer, whose portfolio would also include all of the functional units that deliver value to the customer — marketing, sales, service, product design, R&D, and digital services. In this way, Functional Integration spearheads the process of business transformation required to ensure that the Functional Integration business model captures maximal value for the company.

Nike Digital Sport encounters none of the skepticism that greets early-stage attempts at Functional Integration. It is located on the edge of the Nike campus, with more than 200 employees involved in developing new products and managing the Nike+ platform. In one analyst's estimation, the 55 percent growth in Nike+ membership in 2011 was a key contributor to Nike's 30 percent growth in its running division revenues.[17] Growth of that magnitude used to be achievable with marketing and advertising campaigns; but in the digital age, that level of value capture is possible only through Functional Integration. Far beyond the development and sale of devices such as FuelBand and SportWatch, Nike Digital Sport contributes to Nike's bottom line by cultivating the Nike+ ecosystem and growing the accretive value of the Nike+ membership rolls.

○ Opening Up the Ecosystem

At the start of this chapter, we mentioned in passing how Nokia's Symbian operating system was designed as an open platform that made it easy in 2006 for R/GA and Nokia's marketing division to distribute the viNe application. What we didn't mention was that Symbian's openness had granted Nokia an ideal chance at the time to develop the first-ever smartphone ecosystem of value. Nokia actually considered the idea, and passed.

Although Symbian might seem fairly primitive by today's standards, at the time of its introduction there were software developers around the world who saw it as an exciting new platform — and the only software platform that offered them access to mobile communications. Nokia considered the N-series as a line of handheld computers, and so the company expected third-party software developers to write programs for Symbian as they would for any other computer operating system, such as Microsoft Windows or Apple's Mac.

While working on the viNe project, we saw firsthand the possibilities of the Symbian platform. We also saw that it represented a potentially large competitive advantage for Nokia. All the other cellphone makers had closed their operating systems and restricted the number of available applications to a few very basic and mundane functions. Nokia's phones, by contrast, could become these wonderful customizable devices, different for everyone, with all sorts of useful niche applications that smartphone users couldn't get any other way.

The challenge was that Symbian apps were hard to find and download. The community of software developers who were writing programs for Symbian had a kind of anarchic, hacker ethos that most consumers didn't find appealing or accessible. Nokia, in our view, needed to take the lead in improving the user experience of discovering and downloading apps for Nokia phones. Nokia had the opportunity, well in advance of Apple, of developing an "app store" to aggregate all of the available Symbian apps. However, it seems that no one at Nokia believed there was enough value in such a store to justify the expense. Nokia passed on what would have been the very first app store. When it came to creating a connected ecosystem of value, Nokia missed the boat.

To be fair to Nokia's leadership, though, Apple and Steve Jobs were also somewhat late in realizing the value of third-party smartphone apps. When the iPhone debuted in 2007, the only applications permitted on it were a web browser and a handful of Apple-approved apps for music, photography, maps, weather, and stocks. Despite his reputation as a visionary, Jobs did not really want other people's applications cluttering up his iPhone. He saw the iPhone as an extension of the iPod, which had always offered a closed and very limited menu of functions.

When software developers complained, Jobs pointed out that the iPhone had a web browser. Developers could build whatever they wanted on a mobile web page, and users could save the page to their iPhone home screen. Jobs didn't see how iPhone users and the Apple ecosystem would both benefit from opening the iPhone platform to third-party software.

Within a year, Jobs bowed to pressure inside and outside his organization, and the App Store was born.[18] It was such a success that in 2008 Apple partnered with one of Silicon Valley's premiere venture funds, Kleiner Perkins, to begin the iFund for investment in iPhone app developers. John Doerr, Kleiner Perkins's managing partner, declared at the time that "today we're witnessing history, the creation of the third great platform," in reference to the Mac and iPod as predecessors. "It's bigger," Doerr claimed, "than the personal computer."[19] Portfolio companies in the iFund went on to include Spotify, the Waze traffic app, and Zynga gaming apps.[20] By 2013, the entire Apple App Store had grown to include more than 900,000 apps, contributing an estimated $12.9 billion to Apple's 2013 revenues.[21]

In retrospect, it was Apple's leadership culture that finally allowed iPhone to become connected by design. Even when that leadership was initially reluctant to proceed, the innovation debate continued inside Apple until the company was finally able to embrace a Functional Integration strategy consistent with creating value for users and capturing value for Apple's ecosystem. It didn't hurt that Apple's leadership was already deeply invested in the Apple ecosystem when the debate about the App Store began. The possibilities of future accreted value became too great not to take the step of opening the App Store.

Nokia's leadership culture, by contrast, was just as deeply wed to horizontal integration. Because the operation of an app store did not appear to be a profitable new product by itself, there was no room in Nokia's thinking to recognize how the synergies offered by such a digital service might accrete value that would show up in all Nokia's smartphone sales. When it came to envisioning how a functionally integrated app store might deliver utility, multiple contexts, and synergy, Apple was initially shortsighted, but Nokia was blind.

Nokia's approach to its business as an aggregation of distinct product lines might still be working for the company if Nokia were in the snack food or soft drink business. But Nokia was in the mobile phone business, and the massive disruption that Functional Integration brought to that category in 2008 took everyone by surprise. Even Steve Jobs.

Since then, the debate about ecosystem openness has more or less been closed, although there are a few exceptions. Functional Integration is spreading through the widespread use of APIs (open application programming interfaces), which allow ecosystems of value to grow stronger through the contributions from all kinds of developers. In 2005, Google introduced an API for Google Maps, allowing developers to mash up their own data within Google maps embedded in their websites.[22] By 2013, Google maps were embedded in one million active websites and apps, generating one billion unique visitors every week. The immense popularity of Google's maps, bolstered through its API developer community, has been a key contributor to Google's achievement of all the fundamental Functional Integration principles of utility, multiple contexts, and synergy.[23]

The use of APIs has also emerged as the primary means for connecting software to create new types of services that span the physical and virtual worlds. Nike is giving outside developers access to the real activity data captured from millions of users of Nike+ FuelBand and Nike+ Running devices. Developers use profile and activity data, including NikeFuel points, pace and distance measurements, route records, and running logs, to create new products and services that add value to the Nike+ ecosystem with little effort from Nike itself.

In early 2013, the Nike Digital Sport division launched a start-up accelerator program in which 10 small companies were chosen from thousands of applicants competing for funding and mentorship in creating new products and services as a part of the Nike+ ecosystem. Winners in the competition included a workplace wellness app, an interactive fitness gaming app, and a digital sports coaching platform. Each winner received $20,000 in funding and three months of workspace at Nike headquarters. Some of the winning competitors offered possible future revenue streams for Nike, and provided insights on potential avenues of growth for Nike Digital Sport, such as workplace wellness.[24]

GM in particular should look to Nike's example in building out its new dashboard App Shop ecosystem. Companies with more modest functionally integrated efforts, such as McCormick, L'Oreal Paris, and Progressive, need to consider how they can use open APIs in order to take control of software platforms in their respective categories. If McCormick wants to lay claim to the "flavor" category as its own, if L'Oreal Paris wants to own the beauty category, and if Progressive wants to take charge of driver safety, none of them will be able to achieve these goals by themselves, any more than Apple could have developed 900,000 apps out of its offices in Cupertino.

For all of these reasons, it's important for Functional Integration solutions to be built with an open architecture in mind. The future of scalable business models lies in the connections made among data, software, products, and services. At the heart of every ecosystem is a purpose-built platform for products and digital services to build on each other, adding incremental value over time, adapting and evolving in concert with new user behaviors and new technologies. The burgeoning Functional Integration economy is distinguished by its ethos of openness and collaboration. Organizational traps can be avoided and departmental "not invented here" suspicions can be quelled through APIs and venture funds that help contribute to ecosystem growth and value and eventually deliver a share of growth and brand distinction to the entire enterprise.

o Sustaining (and Sustainable) Success

Ecosystems of value started with technology businesses for the simple reason that technology businesses were already adept at delivering consumer-facing services through technology. The challenge now is for every company to find a way to grow and sustain consumer-facing technologies in the form of Functional Integration, because nearly every business is becoming a tech business.

The rise of the functionally integrated ecosystem as a new business model for brand differentiation and growth should also serve as a vivid reminder that horizontal integration is running out of gas in both respects. Although horizontal integration will be around for some time, it has reached its useful limits in terms of growth. This is good news for business and good news for the planet as well. To understand why, all you need do is examine its inherent wastefulness.

Horizontal integration thrives on waste. The Mad Men vision of everyone buying two cars and living in the suburbs was attractive half a century ago, at least from the perspective of the auto and homebuilding industries. But if that vision had ever come true, it would have been a disaster for the planet. Instead, horizontal integration was always destined to run up against the limits of the resources it consumes, which is what we're seeing today. The low profit margins driven by commoditization are just nature's way of telling us that growth through horizontal integration has had its day.

The most disruptive of all ideas is that of sustainable design. As news readership shifts from print to electronics, demand for newsprint is on a steady decline. Wind and solar power have gotten electric companies frightened that their business model might be broken. And would anyone have predicted at the dawn of the Internet that a generation raised on social media would begin to lose interest in *driving*? Unintended consequences of that kind beg us to imagine what might be coming next.

Functional Integration pushes companies to redefine themselves in terms of the actual value they offer — to others and to the planet. Companies should use Functional Integration as a vehicle for recognizing that their destinies are linked inextricably to the destinies of their customers, which is the ultimate sustainable idea. Thanks to Functional Integration, Nike+ is dedicated to your health and fitness. McCormick FlavorPrint is dedicated to your enjoyment of delicious food. L'Oreal Paris will help you find your best look. Progressive Snapshot might make your child a safer driver.

Using Functional Integration to unlock the value within each company inevitably creates new ways for each of us to unlock potential within ourselves. The ultimate promise of Functional Integration is that it can remind us on a daily basis how everyone and everything on this planet is truly connected by design.

Notes

Introduction

1. Mark McCluskey, "The Nike Experiment," *Wired* 17.07 (June 2009), http://www.wired.com/medtech/health/magazine/17-07/lbnp_nike.
2. Debra Ronca, "How the Nike+ Human Race Works," HowStuffWorks, accessed February 2, 2014, http://adventure.howstuffworks.com/outdoor-activities/running/events/nike-human-race.htm.
3. McCluskey, "The Nike Experiment."
4. Elizabeth L. Bland and Elaine Dutka, "Show Business: Wanna Buy a Revolution?" *Time*, May 18, 1987. Available at http://content.time.com/time/magazine/article/0,9171, 964404,00.html.
5. Cynthia Dagnai-Myron, "The Nike Ad That Changed My Life," *Keka's Blog*, March 16, 2011, http://open.salon.com/blog/keka/2011/03/16/the_nike_ad_that_changed_my_life.
6. Sean Gregory, "Cool Runnings," *Time*, October 4, 2007. Available at content.time.com/time/magazine/article/0,9171, 1668469,00.html.

7. Jay Greene, "How Nike's Social Network Sells to Runners," *Businessweek*, November 5, 2008, http://www.businessweek.com/stories/2008-11-05/how-nikes-social-network-sells-to-runners.

8. Louise Story, "The New Advertising Outlet: Your Life," *New York Times*, October 14, 2007, http://www.nytimes.com/2007/10/14/business/media/14ad.html?pagewanted=all.

9. Gregory, "Cool Runnings."

10. Austin Carr, "Nike: The No. 1 Most Innovative Company of 2013," *Fast Company*, March 2013, http://www.fastcompany.com/most-innovative-companies/2013/nike.

11. Tim Nudd, "How Nike Made 'Just Do It' Obsolete," *Adweek*, June 20, 2012, http://www.adweek.com/news/advertising-branding/how-nike-made-just-do-it-obsolete-141252.

12. "Nike Redefines 'Just Do It' with New Campaign," Nike, August 21, 2013, http://nikeinc.com/news/nike-evolves-just-do-it-with-new-campaign.

13. Apple Inc., "Q4 2013 Earnings Call Transcript," October 28, 2013, http://www.morningstar.com/earnings/58436172-apple-inc-q4-2013.aspx?pindex=2.

14. Jodi Gralnick, "Apples Are Growing in American Homes," CNBC, March 28, 2012, http://www.cnbc.com/id/46857053.

15. Associated Press, "Apple CEO's Compensation Rises Slightly to $4.3M," *USA Today*, December 27, 2013, http://www.usatoday.com/story/money/business/2013/12/27/apple-ceo--tim-cook-compensation/4226267/.

16. "About Amazon," Amazon, accessed February 2, 2014, http://www.amazon.com/b?node=239364011.

17. Nick Wingfield, "More Retailers at Risk of Amazon 'Show-rooming,'" *Bits* (blog), *New York Times*, February 27, 2013, http://bits.blogs.nytimes.com/2013/02/27/more-retailers-at-

risk-of-amazon-showrooming/?_php=true&_type=blogs&_
r=0.

18. "BMW Unveils the Production of i3 in New York, London and Beijing; Efficiency, Dynamics and a Supporting Ecosystem of Services," Green Car Congress blog, July 30, 2013, http://www.greencarcongress.com/2013/07/i3-20130730.html.

19. "Interbrand Best Global Brands 2013," Interbrand, accessed February 1, 2014, http://www.interbrand.com/en/best-global-brands/2013/top-100-list-view.aspx.

20. U.S. Department of Agriculture Economic Research Service, "New Products," last updated February 6, 2013, accessed February 2, 2014, http://www.ers.usda.gov/topics/food-markets-prices/processing-marketing/new-products.aspx#.Ut60Mv30BjA.

21. Clayton M. Christensen and Michael E. Raynor, *The Innovator's Solution: Creating and Sustaining Successful Growth* (Boston: Harvard Business School, 2003), 151.

22. Loizos Heracleous, "Quantum Strategy at Apple Inc," *Organizational Dynamics* 42, no. 2 (April-June 2013): 92–99, http://www.heracleous.org/uploads/1/1/2/9/11299865/quantum_strategy_-_org_dynamics.pdf.

23. James Manyika and others, "Disruptive Technologies," McKinsey Global Institute, May 2013, http://www.mckinsey.com/insights/business_technology/disruptive_technologies?cid=disruptive_tech-eml-alt-mip-mck-oth-1305.

24. Robert Van den Oever, "Philips Exits Consumer Electronics," *Source* (blog), *Wall Street Journal*, January 29, 2013, http://blogs.wsj.com/source/2013/01/29/philips-exits-consumer-electronics/.

25. Hiroko Tabuchi, "Sony's Bread and Butter? It's Not Electronics," *New York Times*, May 27, 2013, http://www.nytimes.com/2013/05/28/business/global/sonys-bread-and-butter-its-not-electronics.html.

Chapter 1

1. John N. Frank, "Cooks Today Are Saying 'Bam!'" *PL Buyer*, November 5, 2010, http://www.privatelabelbuyer.com/articles/83399.

2. Alan D. Wilson, McCormick CEO, quoted in "McCormick's CEO Hosts 'A World of Flavor' Investor Conference (Transcript)," Seeking Alpha, April 17, 2012, http://seekingalpha.com/article/505231-mccormicks-ceo-hosts-a-world-of-flavor-investor-conference-transcript.

3. Elaine Watson, "McCormick on Mission to Become Amazon of Recipes with 'Breakthrough' Flavor Print Application," Foodnavigator-USA.com, April 23, 2012, http://www.foodnavigator-usa.com/Markets/McCormick-on-mission-to-become-Amazon-of-recipes-with-breakthrough-flavor-print-application.

4. McCormick, *Bernstein Strategic Decisions Conference*, May 31, 2013, http://phx.corporate-ir.net/phoenix.zhtml?c=65454&p=irol-presentations.

5. "Facts & Stats," Allrecipes.com, accessed February 2, 2014, http://press.allrecipes.com/fact-stats/.

6. McCormick, *Bernstein Strategic Decisions Conference*.

7. Barb Stuckey, *Taste: Surprising Stories and Science About Why Food Tastes Good* (New York: Atria, 2013), 73.

8. Don Reisinger, "Netflix Gobbles a Third of Peak Internet Traffic in North America," CNET, November 7, 2012, http://news.cnet.com/8301-1023_3-57546405-93/netflix-gobbles-a-third-of-peak-internet-traffic-in-north-america/.

9. "Netflix Recommendations: Beyond the 5 Stars (Part 1)," Netflix blog, April 6, 2012, http://techblog.netflix.com/2012/04/netflix-recommendations-beyond-5-stars.html.

10. Watson, "McCormick on Mission."

11. "R/GA Wins at the 2013 Cannes Lions Festival," R/GA news release, June 19, 2013, http://www.rga.com/news/articles/

cannes-lions-rgas-wins-two-silver-and-one-bronze-for-mastercard-and-mccormick-projects/.

12. Alliston Ackerman, "Leaving a Mark," *Consumer Goods Technology*, November 2013, http://www.consumergoods-digital.com/consumergoodstechnology/november_2013#pg9.

13. Richard Tedlow, *New and Improved: The Story of Mass Marketing in America* (New York: Basic Books, 1990), 110.

14. Matthew Yglesias, "Sweet Sorrow," *Slate*, August 9, 2013, http://www.slate.com/articles/business/rivalries/2013/08/pepsi_paradox_why_people_prefer_coke_even_though_pepsi_wins_in_taste_tests.single.html.

15. "All Brands," Coca-Cola Company, accessed February 2, 2014, http://www.coca-colacompany.com/brands/all/.

16. Yglesias, "Sweet Sorrow."

17. "Wal-Mart Cuts Food Storage Bag Brands," *Store Brands Decisions*, February 9, 2010, http://www.storebrandsdecisions.com/news/2010/02/09/wal-mart-cuts-food-storage-bag-brands.

18. "Walmart to Reverse SKU Count Reductions, Bring Back 8500 Items to Shelves," *Supply Chain Digest*, April 14, 2011, http://www.scdigest.com/ontarget/11-04-14-2.php?cid=4438.

19. Maureen Azzato, "Store Brands Drive Differentiation and Profit," *Store Brands Decisions*, June 13, 2009, http://www.storebrandsdecisions.com/news/2009/06/13/store-brands-drive-differentiation-and-profit.

20. Elaine Watson, "McCormick CEO: We Didn't See as Many New Product Launches from Customers Last Year as We'd Typically Expect," Foodnavigator-USA.com, January 28, 2013, http://www.foodnavigator-usa.com/Suppliers2/

McCormick-CEO-We-didn-t-see-as-many-new-product-launches-from-customers-last-year-as-we-d-typically-expect.

Chapter 2

1. Michael Kwan, "GM Launching App Store Inside Your Car's Dashboard," *Mobile*, April 5, 2013, http://www.mobilemag.com/2013/04/05/gm-app-store-car/.

2. Kevin Fitchard, "GM's Plan to Turn the Car into a Smartphone on Wheels," Gigaom, August 3, 2013, http://gigaom.com/2013/08/03/gms-plan-to-turn-the-car-into-a-smartphone-on-wheels/.

3. Kevin Fitchard, "Is Ford Facing Off Against Apple over the Connected Car?" *Bloomberg Businessweek*, June 12, 2012, http://www.businessweek.com/articles/2012-06-12/is-ford-facing-off-against-apple-over-the-connected-car.

4. Fitchard, "GM's Plan."

5. Ibid.

6. Wayne Cunningham, "Ford Introduces Nine New Apps for the Car at CES 2013," CNET, January 13, 2013, http://ces.cnet.com/8301-34438_1-57562299/ford-introduces-nine-new-apps-for-the-car-at-ces-2013/.

7. William R. Leach, *Land of Desire: Merchants, Power, and the Rise of a New American Culture* (New York: Pantheon, 1993), 42.

8. Alex Kantrowitz, "$70 Billion TV Ad Market Eases into Digital Direction," *Advertising Age*, October 14, 2013, http://adage.com/article/media/70-billion-tv-ad-market-eases-digital-direction/244699/.

9. Don Reisinger, "Worldwide Smartphone User Base Hits 1 Billion," CNET, October 17, 2012, http://news.cnet.com/8301-1035_3-57534132-94/worldwide-smartphone-user-base-hits-1-billion/.

10. Chris Morran, "U.S. Consumers Cut Back Spending on Everything Except Cellphones," *Consumerist*, September 26, 2012, http://consumerist.com/2012/09/26/u-s-consumers-cut-back-spending-on-everything-except-cellphones/.

11. "State of the Appnation — A Year of Change and Growth in U.S. Smartphones," Neilsen, May 16, 2012, http://www.nielsen.com/us/en/newswire/2012/state-of-the-appnation-â%C2%80%C2%93-a-year-of-change-and-growth-in-u-s-smartphones.html.

12. "New CEO.com Study: Twitter, LinkedIn Emerge as Top Social Channels for Business Leaders," Domo, August 7, 2013, http://www.domo.com/news/press-releases/new-ceo-com-study-twitter-linkedin-emerge-as-top-social-channels-for-business-leaders.

13. "How 'I Love Lucy' Dominated Ratings from Its Start," *Hollywood Reporter*, August 15, 2011, http://www.hollywoodreporter.com/news/how-i-love-lucy-dominated-222960.

14. Jim Edwards, "TV Is Dying, and Here Are the Stats That Prove It," *Business Insider*, November 24, 2013, http://www.businessinsider.com/cord-cutters-and-the-death-of-tv-2013-11#ixzz2rDwqOv1G.

15. "New CEO.com Study."

16. Paul Sawers, "Bill Ford: The Automotive and Telecom Industries Are at a Historic Crossroads," TNW blog, February 28, 2012, http://thenextweb.com/mwc/2012/02/28/bill-ford-the-automotive-and-telecom-industries-are-at-a-historic-crossroads/#!q6zDm.

17. Michael Sivak and Brandon Schoettle, "Recent Changes in the Age Composition of US Drivers: Implications for the Extent, Safety, and Environmental Consequences of Personal Transportation," *Traffic Injury Prevention* 12, no. 6 (2011): 588–592.

18. Michael Sivak and Brandon Schoettle, "Recent Changes in the Age Composition of Drivers in 15 Countries," *Traffic Injury Prevention* 13, no. 2 (2012): 126–132.

19. Michael Sivak, "Marketing Implications of the Changing Age Composition of Vehicle Buyers in the US," University of Michigan Transportation Research Institute, Report No. UMTRI-2013-14, May 2013, http://deepblue.lib.umich.edu/ bitstream/handle/2027.42/97760/102946.pdf.

20. "Avis Budget Group to Acquire Zipcar for $12.25 per Share in Cash," Avis Budget Group news release, January 2, 2013, http://ir.avisbudgetgroup.com/releasedetail.cfm?ReleaseID= 731015.

21. Bill Vlasic, "Via Zipcar, Ford Seeks Young Fans," *New York Times*, August 31, 2011, http://www.nytimes.com/2011/08/31/ business/ford-and-zipcar-join-forces.html.

22. Andrew Martin, "Car Sharing Catches On in Avis Deal to Buy Zipcar," *New York Times*, January 3, 2013, http://dealbook .nytimes.com/2013/01/02/avis-to-buy-zipcar-for-500- million/.

23. "Setting Success in Motion," Car2Go, https://www.car2go .com/en/amsterdam/company/. The full updated list of Car2Go cities in Europe and North America appears on a pull-down menu at the upper right-hand corner of this page.

24. Daniel Terdiman, "Viva la Revolucion! Mercedes Channels Che Guevara for Car Tech," CNET, January 10, 2012, http:// www.cnet.com/8301-33369_1-57356306/viva-la-revolucion- mercedes-channels-che-guevara-for-car-tech/.

25. "After One Year, Zipcar Drives Transportation Change in Baltimore," Zipcar press release, July 18, 2011, http:// zipcar.mediaroom.com/index.php?s=25414&item=59719.

26. Yulia Chernova, "Carpooling: Is It Making a Comeback?" *Driver's Seat* (blog), *Wall Street Journal*, July 26, 2012, http://

blogs.wsj.com/drivers-seat/2012/07/26/carpooling-is-it-making-a-comeback/.

27. Niklas Magnusson, "Daimler Acquires 15% of MyTaxi Application for Clicking to Hail a Cab," *Bloomberg News*, January 22, 2012, http://www.bloomberg.com/news/2012-01-22/daimler-acquires-15-of-mytaxi-app-for-clicking-to-hail-a-cab.html.

28. "The New Mobility Platform Moovel," *Technicity* (Daimler), accessed February 2, 2014, http://technicity.daimler.com/en/moovel-mobility-platform/.

29. Stephen Williams, "Report Predicts Auto-Ad Spending Will Grow 14% This Year," *Advertising Age*, April 30, 2012, http://adage.com/article/news/auto-ad-spending-grow-14-2012-forecast/234467/.

30. "Consumers See Fewer Differences Among Car Brands," *Consumer Reports*, January 2012, http://www.consumerreports.org/cro/2012/01/consumers-see-fewer-differences-among-car-brands/index.htm.

31. "RelayRides and OnStar: Baby, You Can Rent My Car," GM news release, July 17, 2012, http://media.gm.com/media/us/en/gm/news.detail.html/content/Pages/news/us/en/2012/Jul/0717_onstar.html.

32. Fitchard, "GM's Plan."

33. Joann Muller, "The Ultimate Driverless Machine," *Forbes*, April 20, 2011, http://www.forbes.com/forbes/2011/0509/global-2000-11-europe-bmw-autos-drivenow-driverless-machine.html.

34. "BMW Smart Key to Replace Wallet," *London Sunday Times*, February 13, 2011, http://www.thesundaytimes.co.uk/sto/ingear/cars/Driving/article543577.ece.

35. "NFC Locking Technology Helps BMW Drivers Book and Then Open Hotel Room," Assa Abloy news release, April 19, 2012, http://www.assaabloy.com/en/com/Press-

News/News/2012/Car-keys-turned-into-mobile-keys-by-VingCard-Elsafe-and-BMW/.

Chapter 3

1. Dennis Sellers, "Mac OS Global Market Share Shows Promise," *PCWorld*, January 9, 2002, http://www.macworld.com/article/1002940/marketshare.html.

2. Walter Isaacson, *Steve Jobs* (New York: Simon & Schuster, 2011), Kindle edition.

3. Austin Carr, "Video: How Steve Jobs's Early Vision for Apple Inspired a Decade of Innovation," *Fast Company*, October 5, 2011, http://www.fastcompany.com/1776369/video-how-steve-jobss-early-vision-apple-inspired-decade-innovation.

4. "Revenue for Apple (APPL) 2001," wikinvest, accessed February 2, 2014, http://www.wikinvest.com/stock/Apple_(AAPL)/Data/Revenue/2001.

5. Michael Kanellos, "Apple Market Share Sinks Again," CNET, December 11, 1997, http://news.cnet.com/Apple-market-share-sinks-again/2100-1001_3-206284.html.

6. Roben Farzad, "Microsoft's Apple Investment: The Worst Deal of Them All?" *Bloomberg Businessweek*, December 9, 2013, http://www.businessweek.com/articles/2013-12-09/worst-deal-ever-microsofts-apple-investment.

7. Leander Kahney, "Straight Dope on the iPod's Birth," *Wired*, October 17, 2006, http://www.wired.com/gadgets/mac/commentary/cultofmac/2006/10/71956?currentPage=all.

8. Charles C. Mann, "The Year the Music Dies," *Wired* 11.02 (February 2003), http://www.wired.com/wired/archive/11.02/dirge.html.

9. Isaacson, *Steve Jobs*.

10. "What's in a Name Change? Look at Apple," *Forbes*, January 25, 2007, http://www.forbes.com/2007/01/25/apple-microsoft-motorola-ent-sales-cx_kw_0125wharton.html.

11. John Borland, "How Sony Failed to Connect, Again," CNET, May 31, 2006, http://news.cnet.com/How-Sony-failed-to-Connect%2C-again/2100-1027_3-6078659.html.

12. Isaacson, *Steve Jobs*.

13. Frank Rose, "The Civil War Inside Sony," *Wired* 11.02 (February 2003), http://www.wired.com/wired/archive/11.02/sony.html.

14. John Paczkowski, "Live from Apple's 'Let's Rock' Event: iPod Updates, Games, Nano Video Cameras," All Things D, September 9, 2009, http://allthingsd.com/20090909/live-from-apples-lets-rock-event-ipods/.

15. "Economic Moats," Morningstar.com's Investing Class-room, Course 205, accessed February 2, 2014, http://news.morningstar.com/classroom2/course.asp?docId=144752&page=1&CN=.

16. Associated Press, "Amazon Kindle, Google Nexus Complicate iPad-Leaning Shoppers' Decision," *Newsday*, December 14, 2013, http://www.newsday.com/business/technology/amazon-kindle-google-nexus-complicate-ipad-leaning-shoppers-decision-1.6602266.

17. "Amazon Has Over 20 Million Kindles in Consumer Hands," CIRP news release, December 11, 2013, http://origin.library.constantcontact.com/download/get/file/1108901228625-83/CIRP+news+release+2013-12-11+Amazon+Kindle.pdf.

18. Jay Yarow, "Amazon Says It Has 20 Million Prime Members," *Business Insider*, January 7, 2014, http://www.businessinsider.in/Amazon-Says-It-Has-20-Million-Prime-Members/articleshow/28490564.cms.

19. Joan E. Solsman, "Netflix Posts Q4 Profit of $48.4M, with 44M Subscribers," CNET, January 22, 2014, http://news.cnet.com/8301-1023_3-57617622-93/netflix-posts-q4-profit-of-$48.4m-with-44m-subscribers/.

20. Jay Greene, "How Nike's Social Network Sells to Runners," *Businessweek*, November 5, 2008, http://www.businessweek .com/stories/2008-11-05/how-nikes-social-network-sells-to-runners.

21. Mark McCluskey, "The Nike Experiment," *Wired* 17.07 (June 2009), http://www.wired.com/medtech/health/magazine/17-07/lbnp_nike.

22. Rosie Baker, "Nike: Digital More Valuable Than Traditional," *MarketingWeek*, June 21, 2012, http://www.marketingweek.co .uk/news/nike-digital-more-valuable-than-traditional/ 4002337.article.

23. Donella H. Meadows and Diana Wright, *Thinking in Systems: A Primer* (White River Junction, VT: Chelsea Green, 2008), 17.

24. Tim Cook, keynote at Apple WWDC 2013, June 10, 2013, http://www.apple.com/apple-events/june-2013/.

25. "App Store Sales Top $10 Billion in 2013," Apple news release, January 7, 2014, https://www.apple.com/pr/library/2014/01/ 07App-Store-Sales-Top-10-Billion-in-2013.html.

26. Steve Jobs, keynote at Apple Special Event, March 2, 2011, http://www.apple.com/apple-events/march-2011/.

27. Theodore Levitt, "Marketing Myopia," *Harvard Business Review*, July-August 1960, 45–56.

28. Sharon Vaknin, "AmazonFresh vs. Supermarket: A Hands-On Shopping Test," CNET, December 17, 2013, http://news .cnet.com/8301-1023_3-57615781-93/amazonfresh-vs-supermarket-a-hands-on-shopping-test/.

29. Baker, "Nike: Digital More Valuable."

30. Austin Carr, "Nike CEO Mark Parker on His Company's Digital Future," *Fast Company*, February 12, 2013, http:// www.fastcompany.com/3005528/most-innovative-companies-mark-parker-nikes-digital-future.

Chapter 4

1. "Bob Metcalfe on What's Wrong with the Internet: It's the Economy, Stupid," *IEEE Internet Computing*, March-April 1997, http://www.computer.org/portal/web/internet/extras/Bob-Metcalf.

2. Peter Grier, "Really Portable Telephones: Costly, but Coming?" *Christian Science Monitor*, April 15, 1981, http://www.csmonitor.com/1981/0415/041506.html.

3. Stephen J. Blumberg and Julian V. Luke, *Wireless Substitution: Early Release of Estimates from the National Health Interview Survey, January–June 2013*, National Center for Health Statistics, December 2013, http://www.cdc.gov/nchs/data/nhis/earlyrelease/wireless201312.pdf.

4. "Activision Blizzard Announces Record Fourth Quarter and Calendar Year 2011 Earnings," Activision company shareholder newsletter, February 9, 2012, http://files.shareholder.com/downloads/ACTI/2691363334x0x541685/787ea4e2-d928-4139-8ae3-4e37250d2443/ATVI_News_2012_2_9_General.pdf.

5. Jeffrey Grubb, "Skylanders Crosses the $1B Revenue Mark with over 100M Toys Sold," *VentureBeat*, February 11, 2013, http://venturebeat.com/2013/02/11/skylanders-crosses-the-1b-revenue-mark-with-over-100m-toys-sold/.

6. "NPD: Spending on Video Games Drops 9%," *USA Today*, February 5, 2013, http://www.usatoday.com/story/tech/gaming/2013/02/05/video-game-content-spending-down-2012/1894551/.

7. Rob Crossley, "Interview: Activision Publishing CEO Eric Hirshberg on the Innovator's Dilemma," *CVG UK*, September 5, 2013, http://www.computerandvideogames.com/427722/interviews/interview-activision-ceo-eric-hirshberg-on-the-innovators-dilemma/.

8. Keith Stuart, "Skylanders Swap Force: 'We Knew We Had a Magical Idea on Our Hands,'" *Games Blog, Guardian*, February 5, 2013, http://www.theguardian.com/technology/gamesblog/2013/feb/05/skylanders-swap-force-eric-hirshberg.

9. Lauren Hockenson, "Parents Prepare: Kids Are Crazy for 'Skylanders Giants,'" Mashable, October 19, 2012, http://mashable.com/2012/10/19/skylanders-giants/.

10. "In-Store 'Sat-Nav' Up and Working Now in a Tesco Branch—Come and Try It!" Tesco blog, May 23, 2011, http://techfortesco.blogspot.com/2011/05/in-store-sat-nav-up-working-now-in.html.

11. Philip Clarke, "Winning Customers in a World of Change," Tesco blog, September 19, 2012, https://www.tescoplc.com/talkingshop/index.asp?blogid=54.

12. Robert Seamans and Feng Zhu, "Responses to Entry in Multi-Sided Markets: The Impact of Craigslist on Local Newspapers," NET Institute Working Paper No. 10-11, May 28, 2013. Available at http://papers.ssrn.com/sol3/papers.cfm?abstract_id=1694622.

13. Andy Robertson, "Confirmed: Disney Infinity Combines Skylanders Toys and Minecraft Creativity," *Wired*, January 15, 2013, http://www.wired.com/geekdad/2013/01/disney-infinity-figures-announced/.

14. Yannick Lejacq, "Toy Story: Interactive Action Figures Are the Latest Video Game Craze," *NBC News*, August 26, 2013, http://www.nbcnews.com/technology/toy-story-interactive-action-figures-are-latest-video-game-craze-6C10970725.

15. Andy Robertson, "'Angry Birds' Telepods Target 'Skylanders' Retail Tower with Their New Special Powers," *Forbes*, September, 18, 2013, http://www.forbes.com/sites/andyrobertson/2013/09/18/angry-birds-telepods-ipad-game/.

16. John Gaudiosi, "Activision CEO Eric Hirshberg Explains the Skylanders Phenomenon," *Forbes*, June 5, 2012, http://

www.forbes.com/sites/johngaudiosi/2012/06/05/activision-ceo-eric-hirshberg-explains-the-skylanders-phenomenon/.

17. Erik Kain, "'Disney Infinity' Review: Playing in the Toy Box on Wii U," *Forbes*, August 27, 2013, http://www.forbes.com/sites/erikkain/2013/08/27/disney-infinity-review-playing-in-the-toy-box-on-wii-u/.

18. "Linking Driving Behavior to Automobile Accidents and Insurance Rates," Progressive Insurance company report, July 2012, http://www.progressive.com/content/pdf/newsroom/Snapshot_REPORT_FINAL_070812.pdf.

19. Ed Arnold, "Progressive's 'Snapshot' Driving Device Worries Consumer Advocacy Group," *Memphis Business Journal*, March 1, 2013, http://www.bizjournals.com/memphis/print-edition/2013/03/01/progressives-snapshot-driving.html?page=all.

20. Nathan Golia, "Consumers 'Receptive' to Telematics, Survey Says," *Insurance and Technology*, September 4, 2013, http://www.insurancetech.com/business-intelligence/consumers-receptive-to-telematics-survey/240160773.

21. Nathan Golia, "Three Things Snapshot Has Taught Progressive," *Insurance and Technology*, September 5, 2013, http://www.insurancetech.com/claims/3-things-snapshot-has-taught-progressive/240160882.

22. "Making Innovation Happen: The CEO's Perspective — Philip Clarke's Speech," Tesco, November 6, 2012, http://www.tescoplc.com/index.asp?pageid=17&newsid=700.

23. Kathy Gordon, "Tesco Rolls Out Budget Hudl Tablet," *Wall Street Journal*, September 23, 2013, http://online.wsj.com/news/articles/SB1000142405270230375960457909278108999 52564.

24. "Majority of U.S. Households Make Purchase Decisions Before Grocery Shopping and Only Occasionally Buy on Impulse, Reports NPD," NPD Group, September 13, 2010,

https://www.npd.com/wps/portal/npd/us/news/press-releases/pr_100913/.

25. Randall Stross, "So You're a Good Driver? Let's Go to the Monitor," *New York Times*, November 24, 2012, http://www.nytimes.com/2012/11/25/business/seeking-cheaper-insurance-drivers-accept-monitoring-devices.html.

26. Leslie Scism, "State Farm Is There: As You Drive," *Wall Street Journal*, August 4, 2013, http://online.wsj.com/news/articles/SB10001424127887323420604578647950497541958.

27. "Progressive Firsts," Progressive, accessed February 2, 2014, http://www.progressive.com/progressive-insurance/first/.

28. "Leading Through Connections," IBM 2012 Global CEO Study. Available at http://www-935.ibm.com/services/us/en/c-suite/ceostudy2012/.

Chapter 5

1. Target Ticket: Kids, accessed February 2, 2014, http://www.targetticket.com/media/kids.

2. Austin Carr, "The First FuelBand Prototype Nike CEO Mark Parker Ever Saw," *Fast Company*, March 18, 2013, http://www.fastcocreate.com/1682588/the-first-fuelband-prototype-nike-ceo-mark-parker-ever-saw.

3. Ibid.

4. David Lieberman, "CEO Forum: Microsoft's Ballmer Having a 'Great Time,'" *USA Today*, April 30, 2007, http://usatoday30.usatoday.com/money/companies/management/2007-04-29-ballmer-ceo-forum-usat_N.htm.

5. David Kilpatrick, "Amazon 'Kindles' Readers' Imagination," *Fortune*, November 23, 2007, http://money.cnn.com/2007/11/19/magazines/fortune/kirkpatrick_kindle.fortune/.

6. "Mission, Vision and Values," Coca-Cola Company, accessed February 2, 2014, http://www.coca-colacompany.com/our-company/mission-vision-values.

7. "From Gray to Green: Watch Coca-Cola 'Roll Out' Happiness in Lithuania," Coca-Cola Company, October 1, 2013, http://www.coca-colacompany.com/stories/from-gray-to-green-watch-coca-cola-roll-out-happiness-in-lithuania.

8. Megan Carter, "Coke Turns a City Square Green, Urges People to Take Off Their Shoes in Latest Campaign," *Fast Company*, October 1, 2013, http://www.fastcocreate.com/3018827/coke-turns-a-city-square-green-urges-people-to-take-off-their-shoes-in-latest-campaign.

9. Brian Whipple and Baiju Shah, "The CMO-CIO Disconnect," Accenture, August 5, 2013. Available at http://www.accenture.com/us-en/Pages/insight-cmo-cio-customer-experience-summary.aspx.

Chapter 6

1. John Battelle, *The Search: How Google and Its Rivals Rewrote the Rules of Business and Transformed Our Culture* (New York: Portfolio, 2005), 91–93.

2. Diane Brady, "Nest's Tony Fadell Keeps His Cool as Google Deal Brings Heat," *Bloomberg Businessweek*, January 22, 2014, http://www.businessweek.com/articles/2014-01-22/nests-tony-fadell-keeps-his-cool-as-google-deal-brings-heat.

3. Aubrey Cohen, "Microsoft Accelerates Kinect-Based Startups," *Seattle Post-Intelligencer*, June 28, 2012, http://www.seattlepi.com/business/tech/article/Microsoft-accelerates-Kinect-based-startups-3671435.php#photo-3132300.

4. Eric Ogg, "Apple Officially Killing Ping Social Network on Sept. 30," Gigaom, September 12, 2012, http://gigaom.com/2012/09/12/apple-officially-killing-ping-social-network-on-sept-30/.

5. "A Second Spring of Cleaning," Google blog, March 13, 2013, http://googleblog.blogspot.com/2013/03/a-second-spring-of-cleaning.html.

Chapter 7

1. "N95 Multimedia Computer Starts Shipping," Nokia press release, March 22, 2007, http://press.nokia.com/2007/03/22/nokia-n95-multimedia-computer-starts-shipping/.

2. Andrew Orlowski, "High-Flying Nokia Now Dependent on Cheapies. Phones? They're What Phones Will Become," *Register*, June 5, 2007, http://www.theregister.co.uk/2007/06/05/nokia_budget_growth_reliance/.

3. Zoe Fox, "Nokia Has Lost 20% of Smartphone Market Since Microsoft Partnership," Mashable, September 3, 2013, http://mashable.com/2013/09/03/nokia-microsoft-partnership/.

4. Juhana Rossi, "Nokia Shareholders Support Handset Sale to Microsoft," *Wall Street Journal*, November 19, 2013, http://online.wsj.com/news/articles/SB10001424052702303531204579208110793654956.

5. "64 Million Smart Phones Shipped Worldwide in 2006," Canalys, February 12, 2007, http://www.canalys.com/newsroom/64-million-smart-phones-shipped-worldwide-2006.

6. "The Institutional Yes," interview with Jeff Bezos by Julia Kirby and Thomas A. Stewart, *Harvard Business Review*, October 2007, http://hbr.org/2007/10/the-institutional-yes/ar/1.

7. Mark W. Johnson, *Seizing the White Space: Business Model Innovation for Growth and Renewal* (Boston: Harvard Business School Publishing, 2010), Kindle edition.

8. Tim Cook, keynote at Apple WWDC 2013, June 10, 2013, http://www.apple.com/apple-events/june-2013/.

9. Don Clark, "Microsoft Takes $900 Million Writeoff on Tablet," *Digits* (blog), *Wall Street Journal*, July 18, 2013, http://blogs.wsj.com/digits/2013/07/18/microsoft-takes-900-million-writeoff-on-struggling-surface-tablet/.

10. "Apple's CEO Discusses F1Q 2013 Results — Earnings Call Transcript," Seeking Alpha, January 23, 2013, http://seekingalpha.com/article/1129431-apples-ceo-discusses-f1q-2013-results-earnings-call-transcript.

11. Warren G. Bennis and Patricia Ward Biederman, *Organizing Genius: The Secrets of Creative Collaboration* (Reading, MA: Addison-Wesley, 1997), 130–135.

12. Carmen Nobel, "Funding Innovation: Is Your Firm Doing It Wrong?" *Working Knowledge*, September 19, 2012, http://hbswk.hbs.edu/item/7025.html.

13. Falk Bielesch, Michael Brigl, Dinesh Khanna, Alexander Roos, and Florian Schmieg, "Corporate Venture Capital: Avoid the Risk, Miss the Rewards," *BCG Perspectives*, October 31, 2012, https://www.bcgperspectives.com/content/articles/innovation_growth_mergers_acquisitions_corporate_venture_capital/.

14. Russ Garland, "Google's Venture Capital Unit Has Busy Third Quarter," *Venture Capital Dispatch* (blog), *Wall Street Journal*, December 19, 2012, http://blogs.wsj.com/venturecapital/2012/10/19/googles-venture-capital-unit-has-busy-third-quarter/.

15. Alexis Tsotsis, "What Happens When Google Wants to Buy a Google Ventures Portfolio Company?" *TechCrunch*, January 14, 2014, http://techcrunch.com/2014/01/14/double-google-all-the-way/.

16. Antonio Regalado, "Money Seeks Idea," *MIT Technology Review*, September 5, 2012, http://www.technologyreview.com/news/428975/money-seeks-idea.

17. Scott Cendrowski, "Nike's New Marketing Mojo," *Fortune*, February 27, 2012, http://management.fortune.cnn.com/2012/02/13/nike-digital-marketing/.

18. Walter Isaacson, *Steve Jobs* (New York: Simon & Schuster, 2011), Kindle edition.

19. Stephanie Olsen, "Kleiner's iFund to Invest in 'Apple Entrepreneurs,'" CNET, March 6, 2008, http://news.cnet.com/8301-10784_3-9887932-7.html?tag=newsmap.

20. For a full list of iFund companies, go to http://www.kpcb.com/companies.

21. Jason Armitrage, "App Store Downloads Exploded in 2012, Apple Says," Yankee Group, January 8, 2013, http://maps .yankeegroup.com/ygapp/content/53219e11218e45ec9831b2 97fc6f35a5/50/DAILYINSIGHT/0.

22. "The World Is Your Javascript-Enabled Oyster," Google blog, June 29, 2005, http://googleblog.blogspot.com/2005/06/ world-is-your-javascript-enabled_29.html.

23. "A Fresh New Look for the Maps API, For All One Million Sites," Google *Geo Developers Blog*, May 15, 2013, http:// googlegeodevelopers.blogspot.com/2013/05/a-fresh-new-look-for-maps-api-for-all.html.

24. Austin Carr, "Nike, Techstars Unveil Startup Accelerator Winners," *Fast Company*, March 19, 2013, http://www .fastcompany.com/3007129/most-innovative-companies-2013/nike-techstars-unveil-startup-accelerator-winners.

Acknowledgments

For giving us the green light to pursue this book, we thank first and foremost Bob Greenberg: leader, visionary, industry legend, gentleman.

The book would not have been possible without the help and advice of our many R/GA colleagues, people who work every day at the cutting edge of business transformation through Functional Integration. Thanks, in particular, to the folks who run the Nike Digital Sport team at R/GA: Jennifer Allen, Nick Coronges, and Wade Convay; the McCormick FlavorPrint team: Andrea Lennon, Katrina Bekessy, Erin Lynch, Karen Bonna-Rainert, Andrew Eaton, Mary Church, Colleen Harlan, Carol Park, Alexandra Leite, and Michael Lewis; and the L'Oreal Paris platform team: Carina Rolley, Erin Lynch, Cindy Pound, Norah Lewin, David Womack, Mary Doyle, Christina Kallery, Micah Topping, and Joe Choi.

Thanks also to our amazing R/GA colleagues Dawn Winchester, Chris Colborn, Stephen Plumlee, John Mayo-Smith, John Antinori, Chloe Gottlieb, Kris Kiger, Richard Ting, Chapin Clark, Taras Wayner, Jay Zasa, Andrea Ring, Dave Edwards, Jess

Greenwood, Nick Law, Jeff Mancini, Luane Kohnke, Sue Davidson, Tony Effik, Dan Kashman, Dan Fradin, Michael Lowenstern, Marc Maleh, John Jones, Micah Topping, Sune Kaae, David DeCheser, Ben Sosinski, Nick Katsivelos, Jennifer Remling, Tim Allen, Isabel Kantor, Anders Erlandsson, Charlotte Ho, Cindy Chastain, Jonathan Greene, James Temple, Jim Moffatt, Paola Colombo, Fabiano Coura, Paulo Benvenuto, Ameer Youssef, and Matt Marcus.

Special thanks go to our amazing clients, whose work is discussed in these pages: Stefan Olander and Ricky Engleberg (Nike); Jill Pratt, Jerry Wolfe, Jennifer LaFrance, and Andrew Foust (McCormick); and Frederic Roze, Marc Speichert, Karen Fondu, Nathalie Kristo, Lisa Capparelli, Kristen Comings, Annamarie Bermundo, Carol Hamilton, and Rachael Johnson (L'Oreal). You are all pioneers of this new business model, and there would be no book if we hadn't done this work together.

The brass at our parent company, Interpublic Group, deserves our thanks for always supporting us in our crazy ventures and ideas—in particular Michael Roth, Philippe Krakowski, and Frank Mergenthaler.

Of course, a special thanks to two people: Karen Murphy, our editor at Jossey-Bass/Wiley, and Noel Weyrich, who helped us organize our thoughts and shape our ideas into a clear narrative.

From Barry

Many people have shaped my ideas and thinking over the 15 years I've spent at R/GA, including all of my aforementioned colleagues. Bob Greenberg deserves special mention because he is the main reason I've never wanted to work anywhere but R/GA. Bob is amazing, which everyone in our industry already knows. We've worked together so long and think so much alike that we often finish each other's sentences. He's a great boss, a good friend, and a source of endless learning and inspiration. He's funny, too, and insanely charming!

My other partner in crime for more than a dozen years at R/GA is Nick Law, our chief creative officer and resident Aussie rogue. Now Nick likes to joke that everyone who works in traditional advertising secretly wishes he or she was working in Hollywood, writing the great American screenplay or directing the next Academy Award best picture. But Nick secretly wishes he was a professional rugby player, knocking the heads of Kiwis and Poms (and just about any other ethnic group he can slur). Somehow he wound up as the world's greatest digital creative director, and somehow I wound up working alongside him trying to figure out how to sell all this crazy digital stuff to clients. We couldn't have been a more perfect match. We are both classic idea-wankers who love to think out loud, argue endlessly, and scrawl stuff on whiteboards — which our good friend David Isaacs turns into the most magnificent presentations. We've both shaped each other's thinking immensely, and I've included some of Nick's thoughts on creativity in this book (cited appropriately).

So many people have influenced and inspired me over the years, from former colleagues to industry gurus. A special shout-out goes to Vin Farrell, Sean Lyons, William Charnock, Danielle Gontier, Ryan Gerber, Ian Spalter, Jill Nussbaum, Ted Metcalfe, Anne Benvenuto, Peter Kim (this book was his idea!), David Shing, David Goodman, Marc de Swaan Arons, Tim Armstrong, Jim Stengel, Brian Perkins, David Bell, Nancy Hill, Rick Boyko, Michael Conrad, Mark Bonchek, Jocelyne Attal, Benjamin Palmer, Megan Pagliuca, Jonathan Nelson, Ana Andjelic, Brian Morrissey, Stacey Lynn Schulman, Alan Schulman, Wendy Lurrie, Gavin McMahon, Rose Fass, Kevin Allen, Howard Draft, Laurence Boschetto, David Mechlin, Pippa Seichrist, Bonnie Lunt, Itamar Kubovy, Lily Binns, Robert Solomon, Steve Thibodeau, Evan Lewis, Lynn Bolger, Mark Avnet, and Heidi Dangelmaier.

Thank you to two guys who taught me just about everything I know about marketing and advertising: Andy Cohen and Brian Cauley, my first two bosses in the agency business. And I must also thank everyone at the Advertising Educational Foundation, Miami Ad School, and Pilobolus. Working with these organizations has motivated me and inspired me more than just about anything else I've done.

From Chris

Thanks to Bob Greenberg for bringing me on to help launch the consulting capability at R/GA. Bob is fearless about deliberately disrupting R/GA's business model every nine years, which is why R/GA is a living, breathing embodiment of business transformation in the face of technological change. It is a great privilege to be starting a new nine-year phase with a leader who practices what he preaches.

I also thank all of my good friends and colleagues at Forrester Research for making me a better thinker and writer, especially David Cooperstein, Josh Bernoff, James McQuivey, Sean Corcoran, Harley Manning, Nate Elliott, Shar Van Boskirk, Sucharita Mulpuru, Christine Overby, Tracy Stokes, Cory Munchbach, Eric Brown, Erin Streeter, and George Colony.

Finally, I thank all of the courageous transformational executives who have, over the years, inspired me with their points of view, shared their war stories, and entrusted me with their challenges: Marty St. George, Wendy Clark, Dana Anderson, Kim Sharan, John Costello, Emilio Pardo, Georges Edouard-Dias, Marc Speichert, Ann Lewnes, Jim Stengel, Kevin Hochman, Rob Price, Marjorie Tenzer, Tim Armstrong, Leigh Zarelli Lewis, Jonathan Tappan, Rebecca Granne, Barry Judge, Rob Malcolm, Pete Krainik, John Gerzema, Paul Gunning, Alex Leikikh, Sarah Hofstetter,

Bryan Wiener, David Jones, Andrew Bennett, Colin Kinsella, David Eastman, Sir Martin Sorrell, Mark Reid, George Rogers, John Wren, Jonathan Nelson, John McGarry, Alan Herrick, Gaston Legorburu, Rei Inamoto, Michael McLaren, Calle Sjoenell, Kenny Tomlin, Dave Knox, Ray Velez, and John Winsor.

About the Authors

Barry Wacksman is executive vice president and chief growth officer at R/GA, a full-service digital advertising and marketing consultancy headquartered in New York, with offices across the United States, Europe, South America, and Asia-Pacific. During his 15 years with R/GA, Barry has helped shape the vision of the agency and advised dozens of Fortune 500 companies on digital strategy. He received a BA in philosophy from Ohio State University and lives in New York with his wife, Alexandra, and his son, Alexander.

Chris Stutzman is managing director of the business transformation practice at R/GA, where he helps companies transform their businesses for the digital age by leveraging technology to create new products, services, business models, and organizational capabilities. Prior to joining R/GA in 2012, he was a vice president and principal analyst at Forrester Research. Chris received an MBA from the Fuqua School of Business at Duke University and a BA in English from Bucknell University. He lives in New York with his wife, Tara, and their son, Finn.

For more information, please visit rga.com.

Index